THE PSYCHOLOGY OF SEX

What can psychology teach us about sex? How do different bodies and brains respond sexually? How can we prevent people being stigmatised for their sexuality?

The Psychology of Sex takes you on a tour through the different ways that psychologists have created and sustained certain understandings of sex and sexuality. Bearing in mind the subjective nature of sex, the book explores cultural concerns around sexualisation, pornography, and sex addiction, as well as drawing on research from sexual communities and the applied area of sex therapy.

When so much of our relationship to sex happens in the mind, *The Psychology of Sex* shows us how important it is to understand where our ideas about sex come from.

Meg-John Barker is a writer, therapist, and activist academic specialising in sex, gender, and relationships. They are a Senior Lecturer in Psychology at the Open University and a UKCP accredited psychotherapist.

THE PSYCHOLOGY OF EVERYTHING

The Psychology of Everything is a series of books which debunk the myths and pseudo-science surrounding some of life's biggest questions.

The series explores the hidden psychological factors that drive us, from our sub-conscious desires and aversions, to the innate social instincts handed to us across the generations. Accessible, informative, and always intriguing, each book is written by an expert in the field, examining how research-based knowledge compares with popular wisdom, and illustrating the potential of psychology to enrich our understanding of humanity and modern life.

Applying a psychological lens to an array of topics and contemporary concerns – from sex to addiction to conspiracy theories – *The Psychology of Everything* will make you look at everything in a new way.

Titles in the series:

The Psychology of Grief
Richard Gross

The Psychology of Sex
Meg-John Barker

The Psychology of Dieting
Jane Ogden

The Psychology of Performance
Stewart T. Cotterill

The Psychology of Trust
Ken J. Rotenberg

The Psychology of Working Life
Toon Taris

The Psychology of Conspiracy Theories
Jan-Willem van Prooijen

The Psychology of Addiction
Jenny Svanberg

The Psychology of Fashion
Carolyn Mair

The Psychology of Gardening
Harriet Gross

The Psychology of Gender
Gary W. Wood

For further information about this series please visit www.thepsychologyofeverything.co.uk

THE PSYCHOLOGY OF SEX

MEG-JOHN BARKER

Routledge
Taylor & Francis Group
LONDON AND NEW YORK

First published 2018
by Routledge
2 Park Square, Milton Park, Abingdon, Oxon OX14 4RN

and by Routledge
711 Third Avenue, New York, NY 10017

Routledge is an imprint of the Taylor & Francis Group, an informa business

British Library Cataloguing-in-Publication Data
A catalogue record for this book is available from the British Library

Library of Congress Cataloging-in-Publication Data
Names: Barker, Meg-John, 1974–author.
Title: The psychology of sex/Meg-John Barker.
Description: New York : Routledge, 2018. | Includes index.
Identifiers: LCCN 2017040560 (print) | LCCN 2017047219 (ebook) | ISBN 9781315560038 (Master e-book) | ISBN 9781138676480 (hardback) | ISBN 9781138676497 (pbk.) | ISBN 9781315560038 (ebk)
Subjects: LCSH: Sex (Psychology) | Sex.
Classification: LCC BF692 (ebook) | LCC BF692 .B347 2018 (print) | DDC 155.3—dc23
LC record available at https://lccn.loc.gov/2017040560

ISBN: 978-1-138-67648-0 (hbk)
ISBN: 978-1-138-67649-7 (pbk)
ISBN: 978-1-315-56003-8 (ebk)

Typeset in Joanna MT
by Apex CoVantage, LLC

CONTENTS

1

PSYCHOLOGY AND SEX

Welcome to the psychology of sex. Like all of the books in the 'psychology of everything' series, a short book like this can't give you a comprehensive overview of the whole of sex and sexuality from a psychological perspective. What it can do, though, is to give you a flavour of this area with the aim of whetting your appetite for more.

Also I hope that, above all else, you'll find this book *useful*. Like it or not we're all living in a world where we're constantly bombarded by sexual information, imagery, and ideologies. Psychology isn't just about finding things out with research, it's also about *evaluating* things psychologically, and *applying* psychology to people's lives. So, in addition to giving you a lot of information about sex from various theories and studies, this book provides you with the tools to think *critically* about the messages you receive about sex and the debates that you see playing out on sexual topics. It also includes a lot about how the psychological research and ideas can be *applied* to people's lives in general, and also to your own life, relationships, and experiences.

Over the five chapters of this book I'm giving you a short introduction to what we know about the psychology of sex across a number of different areas: sexuality (sexual orientation, identity, and attraction); 'the sex act' or sexual intercourse; sexual practices and relationships; and what has recently been called the sexualisation of culture. Each chapter links to various books and papers which you can read to find more about topics you're interested in. I've also given you a list of further resources at the end of the book where you can go to get more information about all of the topics I have covered.

But before we get started on these specific topics let's think a bit more generally about these words we're using: 'psychology' and 'sex'. You might think that it's obvious what they mean but actually they are both rather contested terms. In fact I hope that throughout every chapter of this book you'll continue to ask yourself 'what is psychology?' and 'what is sex?' and that the answers that you give will change as you go along. As with many of the best questions there are no right answers to these, but rather it's important and useful to continually ask them, and to notice how your answers shift as you reflect on them more.

WHAT IS PSYCHOLOGY?

The British Psychological Society, American Psychological Association, and other similar organisations tend to define psychology as something like 'the scientific study of mind and behaviour'.[1] From this we might understand psychology to be one among many scientific disciplines, in this case devoted to researching people's mental processes (mind) and how they act in the world (behaviour). The word 'scientific' might make us think of lab coats, experiments, and measuring these things in *objective* ways using numbers.

The narrow view

Certainly for much of its history psychology has been strongly invested in proving itself to be a science alongside other natural sciences like biology and physics. Students frequently choose a psychology degree because they're interested in people, would like to understand themselves better, or want to help people. So they're often surprised – and not always pleasantly so – by how much of the time they spend learning about mathematical statistics and brain processes!

A lot of the classic kinds of studies that psychologists conduct do seem to support this fairly narrow definition of psychology as the science of mind and behaviour. For example, you might be familiar with the kinds of memory tests that psychologists perform by flashing words up on a computer screen and measuring how many people can remember, examining whether the kind of word, or its place in the list, has an influence on how well it is remembered.[2] Or you may know about Stanley Milgram's classic studies on obedience, where he got people in a lab to think that they were giving somebody gradually increasing electric shocks to help them learn. He found that many people would give somebody a fatal electric shock if somebody in a lab coat told them to do so.[3] Those are two examples of the scientific study of mind (memory) and behaviour (obedience to authority).

I've now been working in psychology for over twenty years. I've been part of several different psychology departments and have many different psychologist friends and colleagues. What I've learned from them is that psychology is actually a good deal broader than what we might at first understand from a definition like 'the scientific study of mind and behaviour'.

The broad view

At its best I think that psychology is the place where all the work which is relevant to our individual human experience comes together. It's a broad, encompassing discipline which draws together all of the knowledge that we have which is relevant to people, and which also looks outwards to address how we can improve people's lives. I have psychologist friends whose work is between psychology and history, psychology and geography, psychology and endocrinology, psychology and sociology, psychology and philosophy, psychology and neuroscience, psychology and criminology, psychology and drama, and many, many more. In fact I know of relatively few 'pure' psychologists. Most study psychology as it touches the edge of at least one other discipline (whether a natural science, a social science, or an arts or humanities subject).

Relatively few of these psychologists conduct lab experiments. Some are entirely engaged with developing theories, others study human behaviour in real-world settings, or interview people in depth about their experiences, or study the history of psychological thinking, or use creative methods to help people produce something that is somewhere between research data and art. Most of them also apply psychological research and theories in some way, informing, for example, the worlds of law, medicine, social justice, counselling, media, or the environment. Some of them work entirely in an applied context, providing therapy, advising organisations, catching criminals, or helping kids in school, for example.

THE PSYCHOLOGY OF SEX

Turning to the subject of this book – or any of the other books in this series – you can see why this broad understanding of psychology is important.

Sex is a fascinating, far-reaching, and fraught area of human experience. We *could* limit ourselves to a narrow view of the psychology of sex and just focus on what we can learn about how people think and behave sexually, from experiments and questionnaires, for example. However, to really reach an understanding of how sex works, how people experience it, and what they think and feel about it, it is important to draw on knowledge from across a wide range of disciplines in conjunction with psychology.

We need to know the history of how people (including psychologists) have understood sex and sexuality, and how that affects how we understand it today. We need to know about the physiology of sex and how different bodies and brains respond sexually. We need to look at sexual identities and practices across cultures and contexts, and at the development of sexual communities and social movements. We need to draw on the wealth of theories that have developed in various branches of philosophy to understand sexuality and sexual relationships. We certainly need to bring the discipline of psychology together with biology and sociology, given that human beings are biological bodies and they all exist in a social context, shaping how they think and behave sexually. And we absolutely need to study the work of the sexologists – people who have studied sex and sexuality specifically over the years – some but not all of whom are psychologists.

And if the psychology of sex is going to be useful at all it also needs to speak to the urgent applied questions that we have about sex: How can we stop people from being marginalised, stigmatised, or even tortured and killed for their sexuality? How can we help people who are experiencing sexual problems? How can we reduce the frighteningly high rates of abusive and coercive sex? How should we treat sexual offenders to stop them committing sex crimes, and help people who have survived such attacks? What would a healthy understanding of sex look like and how might we encourage the promotion of such an understanding in mainstream, social, and sexual media? How should we educate kids about sex? I'm sure you can think of many more.

Psychology is political

One debate that hasn't stopped raging in psychology since the 1970s is whether psychology can be neutral and objective, or whether it is inevitably political: in other words, whether psychologists will have individual and cultural biases which influence what they study, how they study it, and what they find.

This is a vital issue for our purposes here because it influences how I write the rest of this book – and how you read it. Can I present you with a range of research findings and theories from psychology – in its broadest sense – so you can go away with the facts about the psychology of sex? Or will we both need to keep reminding ourselves about how all of the studies and theories we're covering were produced by certain individuals in a certain time and place – perhaps seeing these findings and ideas as *one* way of understanding the psychology of sex, but not as any kind of absolute fact?

Psychologists have often divided into two factions around these kinds of issues. The first faction we might call 'mainstream' psychologists (for want of a better word): those who believe that it's possible for psychology to conduct objective value-free research to determine facts about human minds and behaviour. The latter faction are often called 'critical' psychologists: those who believe that psychological knowledge always develops in a specific situation which will affect what psychologists find and what they do with it. Critical psychologists are interested in how psychologists themselves *construct* knowledge in particular cultural contexts, rather than seeing psychological knowledge as a set of truths that can be uncovered. Knowledge could always have been constructed, built, and shaped in alternative ways.

To overgeneralise quite a lot, mainstream psychologists have also tended to use *quantitative* research to *measure* human minds and behaviours in the form of numbers, and to generalise their findings about the causes and effects of human behaviour to everybody. Critical psychologists have tended to use *qualitative* research to study how people talk about their *experience*, and they're often cautious not to generalise beyond the people they have studied. They're often more interested in *describing* experience than *explaining* it, because they assume that people's experience will vary according to their situation, cultural background, and so on.

In reality this binary mainstream/critical distinction is a false one, and thankfully it is breaking down over the years. Just as I struggled to find examples of colleagues who were entirely 'pure' or 'applied' psychologists, most of the more mainstream psychologists I know tend to be pretty critical in their thinking, and recognise that personal and cultural biases always creep in when human beings are studying other human beings. And I also know a bunch of critical psychologists who use quantitative questions, lab experiments, and brain studies in their work. In this book I'll draw on work across this spectrum.

How psychology is shaped by individuals and their cultural context

A quick tour of the history of psychology shows us how impossible it is to study psychology in a completely objective way. Over and over again studies have found that even when they're trying to be completely unbiased, researchers will tend to find the results that they expect to find. For example, if you give psychology trainees two groups of rats – or children – to study and tell them that one group is more intelligent than the other, then that is exactly what they will find, even when in actuality there's no difference between the two groups.[4] David Rosenhan's classic studies found that psychologists and psychiatrists would diagnose and treat somebody as mentally ill if they were in a mental health institution, even if they showed no signs of mental illness.[5] Clearly our individual expectations shape what we find in research and in professional psychological work.

The history of psychology also throws up some frankly terrifying examples of cultural biases influencing the work of psychologists. In his book *The Mismeasure of Man*,[6] Stephen J. Gould describes the project of intelligence testing to assess US army recruits in the First World War. Using the tests – which were regarded as highly scientifically rigorous – psychologists found that the average intelligence of recruits decreased with the darkness of their skin, with black people and immigrants to the US, including Jewish immigrants, obtaining the lowest scores. At the time, psychologists believed intelligence was entirely inherited, so the researchers concluded that different racial groups had different levels of 'natural' intelligence. These results were used as a basis for limiting immigration, due to fears of immigrants bringing down national intelligence. This prevented around six million Europeans from entering America between World War I and World War II, condemning them to the Holocaust. The research also determined the ways in which army recruits were allocated, effectively condemning many black soldiers to death.

When we look back on this intelligence research now, we recognise many biases which were not seen at the time because the research tallied so well with the prevailing cultural assumptions – in which the researchers were embedded. First, there were a lot of problems with the ways in which the research was conducted, meaning that illiterate and foreign-born recruits were often given tests that required English literacy. Even when that didn't happen, they had to use a pencil, write numbers, and engage in other unfamiliar procedures. Also, many of the questions clearly did not test 'innate intellectual ability'. For example, there were pictures asking recruits to fill in the missing part of a lightbulb, gun, or playing card. And try answering these questions if you're not familiar with US culture: 'Crisco is a: patent medicine, disinfectant, toothpaste, food product?' 'Washington is to Adams as first is to . . .?' Indeed, the research found that foreign-born recruits did better depending on how many years they had been in the US, which should have given the researchers a clue that intelligence was not all down to 'nature'. We'll consider the nature/nurture debate in more depth in the next chapter.

In this example you can see how easy it is for psychologists to perpetuate and reinforce the prevailing views of the time: to divide people into categories on the basis of taken-for-granted knowledge without questioning it, and then to find differences between those categories which they assume are down to innate differences between them, because that is widely held opinion, without looking hard enough for other explanations, or examining the inbuilt biases in the materials they're using.

As Carol Tavris points out in her book *The Mismeasure of Women*,[7] there are many similar examples in the history of the psychology of gender. For example, early research on conformity found that women were more likely to conform than men were. This was used to support the theory that women were naturally intellectually inferior to men. Later research found that women and men are actually much the same when it comes to conformity, and that whether we conform or not has far more to do with how much familiarity we have with the task we're given.[8] Early research had given people tasks that were more familiar to men than women because of the way they were brought up – for example, tasks about machinery. The psychologists then looked no further because the findings confirmed their misogynist assumptions.

You could conclude from these examples that psychologists in the past were biased but now we know so much more we could never make these kinds of mistakes. That would be a dangerous view as it would leave us much more open to making the same kinds of mistakes again. As psychologist Rosalind Gill so succinctly puts it 'you can't step outside of culture' and we need to shine just as much critical light on what we're doing now as we do on the past.[9]

The shaping of the psychology of sex

Certainly when I look across the psychology textbooks in the area of sex and sexuality it's very clear that they're shaped by both prevailing cultural norms and the ways in which the particular psychologists involved situate themselves within those norms. The topics covered, the research and theories which writers deem important to include, and the ways in which these are discussed vary markedly from book to book.[10] I hope that you'll think critically about the stories that I'm telling about the psychology of sex in this book – just as you would with any other book. Like all authors I'm influenced by my own views and experience on this topic, and my cultural context and how I relate to it.[11]

My plan in this book is to tell you about what psychology has discovered about sex and sexuality, and also about how psychology itself has been involved in creating and sustaining certain understandings of sex and sexuality. It's important for you to hold in mind the fact that it does both of these things. In Chapter 2 you'll see that the ways in which psychologists and sexologists have measured sexuality has been influenced by prevailing cultural understandings of sexuality, as well as contributing to those very understandings. In Chapters 3 and 4 you'll see how the diagnostic categories of sexual problems and 'paraphilias' used by psychiatrists and psychologists have changed dramatically over the years: clear evidence of the relationship between psychology and the shifting culture in which it lives. In Chapter 5 you'll explore research and theories produced by psychologists on the different sides of current debates around sexualisation.

WHAT IS SEX?

This is the question that we'll continually be asking over the course of this book as we explore the psychological theories and research in this area, both in terms of what they have contributed to our knowledge about sex, and how they have bolstered or challenged prevailing cultural assumptions.

As with many topics relating to the psychology of everyday life, sex is something that everybody *thinks* they already know about, both from their own experience and from the ideas about sex which circulate in our culture and tend to be taken as fact. For each of the topics I'm exploring here I'll start with this 'common sense' knowledge. What are the taken-for-granteds when people talk about sex, or the popular ideas that are included in sex manuals, TV documentaries, or popular magazines? Then I will unpack the psychological theories and research in the area to examine the evidence for our common sense views, and also to explore the ways in which psychology – and other related academic disciplines – have contributed to our current understandings of sex.

Sex is also a curious topic because it is simultaneously everywhere and nowhere. As you'll see in Chapter 5, there's currently a sense that we're living in a highly sexualised culture, a world saturated with sexual media, advice, and warnings. It's very easy – at the click of a button – to access videos of people having sex, information about any sexual practice or problem, and all kinds of opinions about the latest sex scandal. But at the same time, sex remains hugely taboo. Over the rest of the book you'll see that there's still a vast amount of anxiety about stepping outside the sexual norm, as well as a lot of fear around measuring up sexually and being sexy enough. People don't communicate about sex with health professionals, with their kids, or even with the people they're actually having sex with. And people are still ridiculed, stigmatised, marginalised, pathologised, and criminalised on the basis of their sexual practices and preferences.

For these reasons it's particularly important that psychologists – and other academics and professionals – obtain and promote clear, accurate, and helpful information about sex. It's also vital that they recognise the ways in which their theories and research will be *influenced by* their own experiences and the culture they operate within, as well as the power they have to *shape* that culture and other people's experiences (and the responsibility which goes along with that power).[12]

To summarise what we've said in this chapter, the following diagram illustrates the potential interrelationships between psychology, popular culture, and individual experiences in this area.

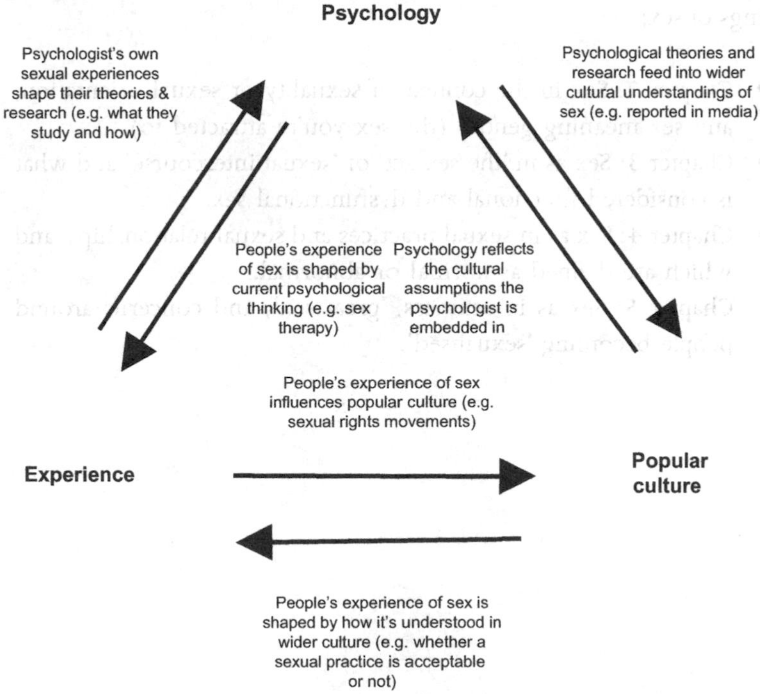
Psychology
Psychologist's own sexual experiences shape their theories & research (e.g. what they study and how)
Psychological theories and research feed into wider cultural understandings of sex (e.g. reported in media)
People's experience of sex is shaped by current psychological thinking (e.g. sex therapy)
Psychology reflects the cultural assumptions the psychologist is embedded in
People's experience of sex influences popular culture (e.g. sexual rights movements)
Experience
Popular culture
People's experience of sex is shaped by how it's understood in wider culture (e.g. whether a sexual practice is acceptable or not)

Figure 1.1 Psychology, popular culture, and individual experience

HOW TO READ THIS BOOK

You might find it helpful to return to this diagram a few times while you're reading the rest of this book because we'll be exploring many examples of the various processes that are summarised here. Many of the examples are historical – because it's often easier to see how such things have happened in the past – but it's vital to keep remembering that they equally apply to the psychology of sex that we're involved in today. In a hundred years' time the work we're doing now may well look just as strange and disturbing to people reading about it as the intelligence testing and gender conformity examples mentioned in this chapter do to us now.

Over the next four chapters we'll consider four different meanings of sex:

- Chapter 2: Sex in the context of sexuality or sexual orientation, and sex meaning gender (the sex you're attracted to).
- Chapter 3: Sex as in 'the sex act' or 'sexual intercourse' and what is considered functional and dysfunctional sex.
- Chapter 4: Sex as in sexual practices and sexual relationships, and which are defined as normal or abnormal.
- Chapter 5: Sex as in sexiness, 'great sex', and concerns around people becoming 'sexualised'.

2

SEX AND SEXUALITY

We tend to see sex as a fundamental aspect of who we are as human beings. A person's *sexuality* is regarded as a vital aspect of their identity: a key piece of demographic information to measure alongside their gender, age, and ethnicity. We think it's important for people to be open about their sexuality: to 'come out' about who they are. And our knowledge or assumptions about a person's sexuality affects our expectations about what they'll be like as a person.

WHAT IS SEXUALITY?

But what do we mean by sexuality? Think for a moment about what your answer would be if you were asked for your sexuality on a form or questionnaire.

Before we get into this chapter let's pull out some of the common cultural assumptions about sexuality. As we do so, you can start to think about whether or not they reflect your understanding and experience of sexuality.

The terms 'sexuality', 'sexual identity', and 'sexual orientation' tend to be used fairly interchangeably, and the latter two terms help to unpack what we generally mean by sexuality. It's a key feature of a person's identity which is defined by who they *orient* towards sexually: in other words, who they are sexually attracted to.

As an *identity*, sexuality is generally assumed to be an *essential* aspect of who we are: part of our fundamental essence as a human being. As such, it's generally assumed to be fixed and unchanging over the course of a life, which is partly why it makes sense to ask it as a piece of demographic information. It's often assumed to be a natural or biological feature of who we are: you were born this way and you'll stay this way.

As an *orientation*, sexuality is all about who we're sexually attracted to in terms of our sex and theirs. Are we attracted to the 'opposite sex' or the 'same sex'? Are we heterosexual or homosexual? There's generally an assumption that people are heterosexual unless they say otherwise. Coming out is associated with gay rather than straight people. Also we tend to ask more questions of people who aren't heterosexual (when did you realise? how do you know? why are you?), suggesting that we generally view heterosexuality as the norm and homosexuality as something other.

Table 2.1 Sexual orientation

		Attracted to	
		Male	**Female**
Person is	**Male**	Homosexual	Heterosexual
	Female	Heterosexual	Homosexual

So, to summarise the common cultural understanding of sexuality:

- Sexuality is *binary* (you're either heterosexual or you're homosexual)
- Sexuality is an aspect of identity whereby we can *categorise* people into one of these two boxes
- Sexuality is *essential*: a feature of who we are which is fixed and unchanging over time
- Sexuality is all about our sex and the sex of people we're attracted to (whether we're male or female and whether we're attracted to males or females)
- Sexuality is a *natural* feature of who we are: something we're born with

PSYCHOLOGY AND SEXUALITY

Many of these ideas about sexuality seem obvious: just something most of us take for granted. However, reading down the list you'll probably have already started to question some of them. You might have thought 'Hang on, what about bisexuality?' or 'I know someone whose sexuality changed in later life', or 'Isn't there a debate about whether it's nature or nurture?'

You'll see in this chapter that psychology has had a major role over the last hundred years or more in shaping these ideas, and in cementing them in the public consciousness. In recent years, however, psychologists have also been involved in questioning these assumptions, and in conducting research finding that sexuality may be a good deal more diverse and complex than this common set of understandings would suggest.

The rest of this chapter takes you through different ways in which psychologists – and other scientists and social scientists – have *measured* sexuality. This will help you to explore each of these assumptions further. It's also a helpful way of demonstrating that the ways in which psychologists define and measure things aren't completely neutral and objective (as we touched on in Chapter 1). Rather, definitions and measurements are often rooted in the wider cultural assumptions which psychologists – as human beings within that culture – tend to accept. Research that's based on these measures often then reinforces these assumptions.

GAY OR STRAIGHT?

The first time that most of us were called upon to think about our sexuality, it was probably framed in this way: 'Are you straight or are you gay?' Up until the point that we found out about these possibilities it's quite likely that we'll have assumed that we – and other people – would be heterosexual, given that the overwhelming majority of books, movies, and teaching materials aimed at kids represent male/female couples and families with mothers and fathers.[1] Just think about the stories, kids' films, and lessons that you remember from when you were growing up. This assumption that people are straight is called *heteronormativity*.

Sadly, most people still learn about the possibility of being something other than straight in the context of that alternative being a negative (or at least strange) thing. The word 'gay', and derogatory terms for homosexuality, are still popular playground insults.[2]

This idea that people are heterosexual or homosexual isn't how people have always understood sexuality though. Historians of sexuality talk about 'the invention of homosexuality' in the nineteenth century. If you'd lived before that time it wouldn't have made sense to you to think of a person as gay – or as straight either.

Early sexology

Towards the end of the nineteenth century various scholars began the project of classifying and categorising sex. At that point psychology was still in its infancy, and many of the early sexologists were psychiatrists or other kinds of medics rather than psychologists as such. Sexologists such as Richard von Krafft-Ebing, Magnus Hirschfeld, and Henry Havelock Ellis, applied the approach of classification which was popular in medicine and science to the field of sexuality. Generally they attempted to categorise different types of sexual deviance.

We'll return to the importance of early sexology in shaping our thinking about sex in terms of normality and abnormality in Chapter 4. What's important for our purposes here is that these classifications started a shift from sexuality being seen as something you *did*, to something you *were*. Before that time some sexual behaviours – such as sodomy – had been regarded as a sin or a crime, but not as something that made you a certain type of person. That's why we can talk about the 'invention' of homosexuality – and heterosexuality. Before that time a person wouldn't have been seen as a homosexual or a heterosexual.

This understanding of sexuality as an identity has had a marked impact on how people have been treated ever since. It meant that people could now be discriminated against, criminalised, and pathologised on the basis of their sexuality: being seen as a fundamentally bad, wrong, or sick kind of person. It also meant that people could fight for rights; their sexuality made them a certain kind of person who should be treated equally to everyone else. Indeed, some of the first sexologists were involved in the earliest versions of the gay rights movement.

Freud and psychoanalysis

The famous father of psychoanalysis, Sigmund Freud, was responsible for developing the ideas of the early sexologists, and planting them clearly in the popular imagination. While most of the early sexologists believed that there were biomedical explanations for a person's sexuality, Freud believed that sexuality was something that developed over time. Freud was still *essentialist*, however, because he saw sexuality as a fundamental feature of who a person was which was fixed by the time they became an adult.

Freud believed that there were two key aspects of sexuality: the sexual *aim* and the sexual *object*. We'll return to the sexual aim in the next chapter because that's about the parts of the body that we get sexual satisfaction from.

Freud's theory of the sexual object was vital for setting in stone the gay/straight binary that we're exploring here. His theory held that people were born 'polymorphously perverse' and capable of attraction regardless of a person's gender. However, through a set of developmental stages they came to a mature sexuality. Freud theorised that people reach a stable sexual *object choice*: attraction to the opposite sex after going through the Oedipus complex. This involves coming to identify with the same-sex parent after having previously desired their opposite-sex parent and seen the same-sex parent as a rival. Not going through the Oedipus complex fully could leave someone attracted to the same sex.

So we can see that the early sexologists and psychoanalysts set the blueprint for how we think about sexuality today: as a fundamental aspect of our identity and as a binary: being attracted to the same or opposite sex.

Psychology and the straight/gay binary

Most mainstream psychologists today have little time for Freud's theories – regarding them as unscientific to say the least![3] However, the idea that people have an inherent sexual orientation towards the same or opposite sex has remained relatively unchallenged.

A few years back I reviewed the main psychology textbooks at the time to see how they covered sexuality.[4] I found that this topic was almost exclusively covered in the biological psychology sections of textbooks – and indeed the dominant way of understanding sexuality has definitely swung back from nurture to nature since Freud's day. Most of the textbooks covered sexuality in the same way: in a section covering (mostly biological) explanations for why some people are gay. Particularly common was the search for the 'gay gene' and associated research on differences between straight and gay people that might suggest a genetic cause. We'll touch on this again later when we return to the nature/nurture question.

What you can see from this analysis is that it's still very common in psychology to regard sexuality as fixed and binary, with heterosexuality being the assumed norm, and homosexuality therefore requiring some kind of explanation for its existence.

Invisible bisexuals in psychology

It is important for what we're thinking about here that I found very little mention of the possibility of bisexuality in psychology textbooks. Half didn't acknowledge its existence at all, asking questions like 'Why do some people prefer partners of the other sex and some prefer partners of their own sex?' with no recognition that some might prefer either or both. The other half of the books touched on bisexuality very briefly, and then went on to cover only theories and research relating to straight and gay people. Often these mentions of bisexuality happened in order to downplay it: either arguing that it didn't exist at all, or that it was extremely rare.

This questioning of bisexuality as a legitimate sexual orientation has been common in psychology in recent decades. Many psychologists have insisted that sexuality is binary and that therefore bisexuality cannot exist.

One particularly famous study was reported in the *New York Times* as proving that bisexual men were 'straight, gay, or lying'.[5] It claimed to have found that men who identified as bisexual actually responded only in a 'homosexual' or 'heterosexual' manner.[6] In this study men who identified as gay, straight, or bisexual were wired up to a *penile plethysmograph* device, which measures the extent of erection in the penis. They were then shown pornographic films of two men having sex or two women having sex. Around a third of the participants didn't respond sufficiently to either stimulus to be included in the data analysis. Of those remaining they generally either responded to the first movie, or to the second, but not to both. You might want to pause for a moment to consider what you think of this study. Is measuring physiological arousal a good way at getting at a person's 'true' sexual orientation? Do you agree that it supports the conclusion that bisexual attraction doesn't exist?

The study was criticised for several reasons. Certainly we might question whether people are 'homosexually attracted' if their penises responded to images of two men having sex, and 'heterosexually attracted' if their penises responded to images of two women having sex. Obviously the researchers wanted to avoid having pornography with a man and a woman in it, because the results would be unclear, but are all heterosexual men attracted to two women together? Would we conclude that a woman was heterosexual if she responded to a film of two men together? Also it seems possible that many bisexual men may well have been excluded from the study as part of the group who didn't show sufficient arousal to either film to be included.

Interestingly the study was repeated by the same research laboratory a few years later.[7] After taking on board the criticisms, the lab did then find participants who showed a pattern of bisexual attraction. This represents a wider shift in psychology towards acknowledging the existence of bisexuality, although there is still slow progress in breaking down binary assumptions.

Culturally the binary understanding of sexuality seems very embedded and bisexuality is still frequently represented in the media as questionable, suspicious, 'just a phase', or not existing at all. Psychological research on mental health which does tease out bisexual experience overwhelmingly finds that bisexual people experience worse mental health than heterosexual or lesbian and gay people. This has been linked to the fact that bisexual people are frequently denied or stigmatised because of their sexuality.[8] We might ask ourselves what it was like to live as a bisexual man in the years between the original study and the repeated version – when it was commonly held that science had proved that they were really gay, straight, or lying.

CATEGORIES OR CONTINUUM?

So we've seen that there's generally agreement in psychology these days that sexuality isn't binary, and that this is slowly filtering into popular culture. For this reason, studies of sexuality – like the ones I just mentioned on mental health – would tend to now include a demographic scale that included *three* categories for sexuality. To see what that might look like, here's the current demographic scale of sexual orientation suggested by the Equality and Human Rights Commission.[9]

Demographic categories

Which of the following options best describes how you think of yourself?

Heterosexual or straight ☐
Gay or lesbian ☐

Bisexual ☐
Other ☐
Prefer not to say ☐

You might like to pause and think for yourself which box you'd tick here. What kind of demographic data does it capture, and what's missing from it, in relation to understanding a person's sexuality?

In answer to this question you might have considered that these sexual orientation labels give us a good sense of how a person defines themself but not necessarily much of a sense of this person's actual behaviours or attractions. This is one of the issues that penile plethysmography and vaginal photoplethysmography studies are attempting to address. For example, somebody might have had sexual experiences or attractions to more than one gender but still label themselves as straight or gay, perhaps because they're worried about homophobia (if they identify as straight) or because they feel that they're part of a gay community (if they identify as gay) and don't want to be rejected by that community.

The idea of identifying yourself as a certain sexual orientation is also culturally specific: not all cultures and communities do this. Finally, there are only three options here: heterosexual, bisexual, or gay. You might wonder whether that covers the diversity of people's sexual attraction. We'll come back to this shortly.

So what other ways might there be of measuring a person's sexuality if we recognise that identity labels don't completely capture it? One example that you've probably heard of is the Kinsey scale. This takes the recognition that sexuality isn't binary a stage further than adding an additional category of bisexual between homosexual and heterosexual: it imagines sexuality on a *spectrum* or *continuum*.

Alfred Kinsey was a biologist working in the US in the 1940s. He noticed the negative impact that the massive cultural taboos and ignorance around sex at the time had on him and on the students he taught. Some of this was a legacy of the sexologies of deviance and psychoanalytic theories that we looked at earlier. For this reason Kinsey set out to study sex scientifically: to inform everyone about what people were really doing sexually. Two books were published based on his team's extensive sex history interviews with thousands of people, *Sexual Behavior in the Human Male* and *Sexual Behavior in the Human Female*. These are popularly known as the Kinsey Reports and became instant bestsellers.[10] Among other findings which shook cultural assumptions about sex to their foundations, the Kinsey research found that 92% of men and 62% of women had masturbated, 70% of couples engaged in oral sex and 11% anal sex, and between 67% and 98% of men and around 50% of women had had sex before marriage.[11]

What is of most interest to us here, though, is the Kinsey scale. Because Kinsey was interested in behaviour rather than identity, instead of asking people their sexuality he placed them on a continuum from exclusively heterosexual to exclusively homosexual on the basis of their sexual experience.

The Kinsey scale

0 exclusively heterosexual
1 predominantly heterosexual, only incidentally homosexual
2 predominantly heterosexual but more than incidentally homosexual
3 equally heterosexual and homosexual
4 predominantly homosexual but more than incidentally heterosexual
5 predominantly homosexual, only incidentally heterosexual
6 exclusively homosexual
X No sexual attraction

On the basis of this, Kinsey found that 2% to 6% of women and 4% of men were exclusively homosexual. A range of 6% to 14% of women and 46% of men had had both heterosexual and homosexual experiences, and 13% of women and 37% of men had had at least one homosexual experience to the point of orgasm.

Pause for a moment and consider where you'd fall on the Kinsey scale. Did you have any trouble deciding? What do you think the Kinsey scale captures and what's missing from it, in relation to understanding a person's sexuality?

The Kinsey scale is based on experience rather than identity, and it gets at a range of experiences. This is important because we get very different statistics when we ask about sexual identity to when we ask about sexual experience. Looking across all of the US and UK studies, over three times as many people say they've had at least one same-sex sexual experience as those who claim identity as lesbian, gay, or bisexual (LGB). In the most up-to-date UK example while I was writing this book, the surveying company YouGov found that 88.7% of adults identified as heterosexual, 5.5% identified as gay, and 2.1% as bisexual. When they were asked to place themselves on the Kinsey scale, however, 72% of all adults, and 46% of adults aged 18–24 years, put themselves at zero; 4% of all adults, and 6% of young adults, put themselves at six. That means that a quarter of all adults, and half of young adults, placed themselves somewhere between the extremes. This is a fascinating statistic to consider alongside the long-held cultural and psychological view that bisexuality doesn't exist or is extremely rare.

Kinsey's research has been criticised for the ways in which the data was collected and analysed – which makes it difficult to tell whether the findings were representative of the whole population. Again, this alerts us to the fact that the ways in which psychologists – and other scientists – study sex and sexuality has a marked impact on what they find. The shifting numbers over the years, across different studies, cultures and generations, also suggest that there is some social element to how we experience, identify, and report on our sexuality – something we'll return to towards the end of this chapter.[12]

While Kinsey's findings were based on people's reported sexual behaviour, it isn't completely clear whether the YouGov survey respondents are talking about their experience or their attractions. This diagram helps us to think about how the proportions are likely to differ depending on the question we're asking.

Identity, experience, attraction

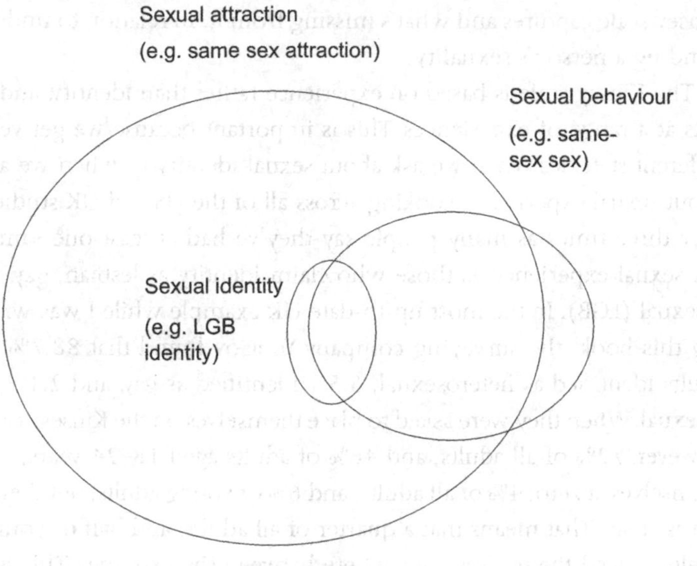

Figure 2.1 Sexual identity, behaviour, and attraction

For any aspect of sexuality the greatest proportion of people are likely to have that attraction without necessarily acting on it or identifying with it. A smaller subset will behave in that way, and a smaller subset will identify that way. The overlaps on the diagram are because some people will identify with a sexuality without necessarily having acted upon it (young people and celibate people, for example), and some people will sometimes behave in a way that doesn't match their sexual attraction (some actors, sex workers, and people learning about their sexuality, for example).

Another drawback of the Kinsey scale – at least as it was used in the YouGov survey – is that, like demographic identity terms, it only gives us a snapshot of how somebody sees their sexuality at the point in time that they are doing the survey. Therefore, if we're not careful, research like this – which takes place at one point in time and relies on a single measure – can give the impression that sexuality is a relatively static, fixed thing – without actually checking whether that is the case.

FIXED OR FLUID?

Fritz Klein, a US sexologist and psychiatrist who followed Kinsey, came up with this grid for studying sexuality, due to the problems I just mentioned with the Kinsey scale.[13] You might like to have a go at filling it in yourself, or just think about whether it is a better or worse measure than Kinsey's.

You might notice that this scale gets at sexual attraction, behaviour, *and* identity, rather than only studying one of these. It also captures some additional dimensions to sexuality, such as political identity, which may differ from sexual identity. For example, somebody could be very involved in LGB rights without necessarily being LGB themselves, perhaps due to friends or family members being LGB. It also builds in the important possibility that all of these aspects might change over time, rather than regarding sexual experience or identity as fixed and static. Research using this grid has found that the numbers people give for each dimension often do vary across time.[14]

Sexual fluidity

Klein's theory that sexuality could be dynamic did not catch on immediately when he was writing about these matters in the 1980s, and certainly the Klein grid never gained the kind of popular attention that the Kinsey scale has received. Recent years, however, have seen renewed attention to the concept of dynamic sexuality or *sexual fluidity*. A key researcher in this area is Lisa Diamond.[15] Diamond studied a hundred women who experienced some degree of same-sex attraction over the course of a decade. She found that around two-thirds of the women changed their sexual identity label at least once during this period, and in all possible directions (lesbian to bisexual, bisexual to heterosexual, unlabelled to lesbian, etc.). These changes

Table 2.2 The Klein grid

	Terms	**More than 10 years ago**	**More than 5 years ago**	**More than a year ago**	**In the past year**	**In the future**
1	Sexual attraction – who turns you on					
2	Sexual behaviour – who you have sex with					
3	Sexual fantasies – who you have sexual fantasies about					
4	Emotional preference – who you have strong emotional bonds with					
5	Social preference – who you like to spend your leisure time with					
6	Lifestyle – the sexual identity of the people you spend time with					
7	Sexual identity – how you self identify					
8	Political identify – who you identify with					

Scale used for rows 1–5: 1 = Other sex only, 2 = Other sex mostly, 3 = Other sex somewhat more, 4 = Both sexes equally, 5 = Same sex somewhat more, 6 = Same sex mostly, 7 = Same sex only, 0 = Does not apply

Scale used for rows 6–8: 1 = Heterosexual only, 2 = Heterosexual mostly, 3 = Bisexual mostly, some hetero, 4 = Bisexual only, 5 = Bisexual mostly, some homo, 6 = Homosexual mostly, 7 = Homosexual only

often coincided with the gender of their current sexual or romantic partners. Diamond concluded that this demonstrated sexual fluidity: the capacity to adapt sexual and romantic attraction to a specific person instead of to an overall gender category.

Since Diamond's initial study there has been a lot of focus on gender differences in sexual fluidity, with many psychologists suggesting that women are more sexually fluid than men. For example, going back to the physiological arousal studies that I mentioned earlier, Meredith Chivers and colleagues found that women tended to respond genitally to all kinds of depictions of sex acts (including those between men and women, between women, and between animals), whereas men responded more specifically depending on the gender of the people they were watching (in line with their sexual orientation).[16] Like Diamond, Ritch Savin Williams and his colleagues conducted a study of sexual identity over time and found that men's identity labels were less likely to change than women's.[17] However, another national US survey found that half of men with a bisexual identity showed identity change over time, so being male doesn't necessarily mean having a rigid or fixed sexuality.[18]

While some researchers argue for some fundamental gender difference to explain these kinds of findings, it's also important to consider the role of cultural homophobia and biphobia here. Masculinity is still strongly defined against femininity and homosexuality in much of society[19]: being a 'real man' means not being feminine and not being gay. In support of cultural involvement, another study of men who had sex with men found that more of them identified as straight than gay, and almost none as bisexual.[20] Whatever the reason, it seems clear that some people experience their sexuality as relatively fixed over time, and some as rather more fluid and changeable.

You might find it helpful to reflect on which aspects of your sexuality, and which kinds of people you find attractive (if any), have changed over time, and which have stayed relatively stable. It's important to emphasise here that sexual fluidity doesn't equate to 'changeable at will'. While some people have found that different sexual experiences open up attractions and arousal patterns that they hadn't realised were possible, endeavours to change a person's sexuality – usually to conform to a more culturally acceptable pattern – have overwhelmingly failed and are ethically highly questionable.[21]

ALL ABOUT SEX?

There's one more thing that you might have noticed across all the research we've explored here so far, whether it has used demographic lists, or continuums, or physiological arousal measures. In fact you might *not* have noticed it because it is taken for granted by most psychologists. That is the assumption that sexuality – whether identity, experience, or attraction, and whether fixed or fluid – is all about the sex of the person we're attracted to. Even the Kinsey scale and the Klein grid assume that the defining feature of a person's sexuality is the extent to which they're attracted to the same sex or the opposite sex.

There are two issues with this. First, like sexual orientation, sex and gender are not binary, so the 'same or opposite' distinction we've been using is problematic. Second, it fails to account for all of the other features of a person's sexuality which might be as important, or even more important, than the sex or gender of the people they find attractive or have sex with.

Sex/gender

Psychologists often use the word 'sex' to refer to our biological features, and gender to refer to whether somebody takes on the roles and behaviours which are socially associated with masculinity or femininity (or both or neither). Actually it's a lot more complex than this because there are a whole lot of different aspects of our biological, psychological, and social sex/gender, and none of these are simply binary (male or female).

Starting with biology, there's diversity across all levels of sex/gender. There is diversity in chromosomal makeup, in hormonal sensitivity and take-up, and in genitals (so it's not always clear what is a penis or a clitoris). There's also diversity in all of the physical aspects which we tend to regard as 'male' or 'female', with many people fitting better on the 'opposite' end of the spectrum than we might predict by gender stereotypes (height, voice pitch, strength, hairiness, and chest size). As geneticist Anne Fausto-Sterling puts it:

> While male and female stand on the extreme ends of a biological continuum, there are many bodies . . . that evidently mix together anatomical components conventionally attributed to both males and females. . . . Modern surgical techniques help maintain the two-sex system. Today children who are born 'either/or–neither/both' – a fairly common phenomenon – usually disappear from view because doctors 'correct' them right away with surgery.[22]

Recent research has shown that brains too are not binary. Neuroscientist Daphna Joel and colleagues found that the idea of the 'male' and 'female' brain is a myth: between 0 and 8% of people have all of the brain features they might be expected to have, based on their sex. The vast majority of people have some combination of these features.[23] Another neuroscientist, Cordelia Fine, has also emphasised *neuroplasticity*: the fact that many of the gender differences that *are* found in the brain are due to the way in which people have learnt gender roles – meaning that certain neural connections have been made and not others.[24] Gendered brain differences are often a product of gender experience, rather than a cause of it.

It's not surprising, then, that globally many cultures recognise more than two genders.[25] Despite the tendency in the west to view gender as binary, as with sexuality things seem to be starting to shift here too. You might be familiar with the range of gender identity terms that social media site Facebook now offers: up to 71 different possibilities at the time of writing, including options such as bigender, gender neutral, androgynous, genderqueer, and gender fluid. According to official statistics, the proportion of the UK population who define as non-binary when given an option beyond male and female is around 1 in 250 people.[26] In another study by Daphna Joel and colleagues, they found that, in a general population, over a third of people said that they were to some extent the 'other' gender, 'both genders' and/or 'neither gender'.[27] You might pause and think to yourself whether you, or the people you know, fit perfectly into the cultural stereotypes of masculinity or femininity.[28]

As with sexuality, some people experience their gender as very fixed, some as fluid and changing; and everything in between is also represented. For some (cisgender) people the gender that they are assigned at birth – generally on the basis of their genitalia – fits their experience of their gender, for other (trans) people – including non-binary people – it does not.

Going back to the diagram of our cultural understanding of sexual orientation earlier in this chapter, you saw how it assumes both sexuality and gender to be binary (male/female, gay/straight), but perhaps these binary categories have been imposed on a human experience that isn't binary at all. If that is the case then any measure of sexuality that assumes that there are two, and only two, genders that a person could be attracted to (same, opposite, or some degree of both) is going to be flawed.

Focus on sex/gender of attraction

There's another perhaps even more significant problem here: the importance placed on both gender and sexual orientation in defining a person. Psychologist Sandra Bem raised the question of why gender is seen as such an important feature throughout her work. She argued that gender was not useful as an organising category and that psychology – and wider culture – should move away from the use of gender categories entirely.[29] The same could be said for sexual orientation. If you remember back to Lisa Diamond's work, she found that for many of the women she studied, their sexuality was much more about the person they found attractive, or had a relationship with, than their gender.

This accords with research on bisexual people which has found that many define bisexuality as being attracted to people 'regardless of gender,' seeing gender as a feature of potential partners that is no more important than eye colour, for example.[30] It also makes sense of the way in which sexual identity terms have exploded in recent years – in a similar way to the gender terms on Facebook. Younger people are increasingly using multiple terms to describe their sexuality, including pansexual, queer, kinky, polyamarous, asexual, sapiosexual, scoliosexual, and many other terms.[31]

Some psychologists – and other social scientists – study sexuality more *qualitatively* than *quantitatively*: asking people with certain sexualities to describe or discuss their experience, rather than trying to capture it in numbers. They often find there is very little focus on gender of attraction when you approach it in this way. Rather, people talk in much more depth about other aspects related to their sexuality: such as their sense of belonging to a social group and ability to 'be themselves',[32] or the rich detail of their specific sexual fantasies and experiences.[33]

Sexuality theorist Eve Kosofsky Sedgwick comments on the narrow focus on sexual orientation, saying,

> it is a rather amazing fact that, of the very many dimensions along which the genital activity of one person can be differentiated from that of another (dimensions that include preferences for certain acts, certain zones or sensations, certain physical types, a certain frequency, certain symbolic investments, certain relations of age or power, a certain species, a certain number of participants, and so on) precisely one, the gender of the object choice, emerged from the turn of the century, and has remained, as the dimension denoted by the now ubiquitous category of 'sexual orientation'.[34]

Think about it yourself. Can the important features of your sexuality be captured in a term relating to which gender you find attractive (bisexual, gay, straight, etc.) or would you need to describe other things – for example if you were searching for somebody who might be sexually compatible on a dating website. You might want to consider, for example:

- The kinds of people you're attracted to in terms of other aspects such as physical appearance, age, personality, clothing, etc.
- The kinds of situations, images, roles, activities or fantasies, if any, which excite you – and turn you off – physically and/or psychologically.
- The kinds of physical sensations you enjoy and don't enjoy.

Sexual configurations

Biological psychological research has recently begun to consider multiple dimensions of human sexuality rather than limiting itself to orientation on the basis of gender. In her framework for human sexuality Sari Van Anders[35] reviews the biological and psychological research relating to the following dimensions:

- The physical sex of the person we're attracted to,
- Their gender (how masculine, feminine or androgynous they are, which may or may not match their physical sex), and
- The number of people we can be attracted to at the same time (whether we're monogamous or non-monogamous or something in between, see Chapter 4).

Van Anders also acknowledges that there are probably many more possible dimensions, and we'll be considering a few of them over the coming chapters (particularly the level of sexual attraction we experience – from none to high, and where we are on spectrums of sexually submissive/dominant, or passive/active).

So in order to measure sexuality completely we'd need something far more complex than a Kinsey scale, or even a Klein grid. We'd need to imagine something like multiple Kinsey scales on these many different dimensions all intersecting and interweaving in complex ways. And if that's not already complicated enough, sexual fluidity means that where we are on these dimensions is probably shifting and changing over time. And – as Van Anders and Diamond point out – we may be in different places in terms of who we are sexually attracted to (if anyone), what we think about during solo sex (if anything), and who we have emotionally close or romantic relationships with (if anyone). We all have a unique *sexual configuration*, rather than a sexual orientation that we share with a large proportion of the population.

NATURE, NURTURE, OR . . . SOMETHING ELSE?

Now that we've explored how we understand sexuality, let's return to the other question about sexuality which has vexed psychologists (and other scientists) since the start: the question of what *causes* our sexuality.

If you remember back to the beginning of this chapter you'll remember that the questions of categorisation and causation were pretty much interlinked in early theories of sexuality. The first sexologists assumed that the sexual 'deviants' they classified were explainable by biological variation. Freud theorised that adult sexuality could be explained by people becoming fixated at one of the early stages of childhood sexual development and therefore not having developed to 'healthy' sexual maturity. In the last few decades the prevailing view has swung back to biology with the search for the 'gay gene' and for brain differences to account for sexual orientation.

These shifts demonstrate the way in which the question has often been put – in psychology and in wider culture – as 'nature or nurture?' Are gay people born that way, or made that way? By now I hope you can already see that there are problems with the way in which this question is framed, which will mean that any research attempting to answer it will be of limited value.

Problems with the question

First, framed in this way the question assumes that there is normal sexual orientation (heterosexuality), and then there is sexual orientation which is different from that (homosexuality), and that requires explanation. Otherwise we'd be asking what caused heterosexuality too. As we've seen throughout this chapter, however, sexuality isn't binary. Even if we could pull out one dimension (gender of attraction) to focus on in this way, we'd need to account for the whole spectrum of possible attractions and their lack rather than just attempting to explain one end of the spectrum.

Second, the question of causation often assumes that there will be *one* explanation that accounts for all people who have a certain sexuality. Why are people gay? Why are people bi? These may sound like reasonable questions because we've heard them asked in that way so many times. As we'll see in later chapters the same tends to apply when psychologists search for explanations of other sexual identities and practices. Returning to what we learnt from Klein and Van Anders, we can see a problem with this. If – as seems to be the case – each of us has a unique sexual configuration where we sit in different places on a number of different dimensions, then it seems unlikely that we could find universal explanations for sexuality. It's more likely that multiple elements are involved in shaping our sexuality, operating together in complex ways that differ from person to person. In addition to that, of course, we need explanations that can account for the shifts and changes that many people experience over time – sexual fluidity – as well as the experiences of those whose sexuality seems to be more fixed.

Sedgwick, who we encountered earlier, has pointed out that the nature/nurture binary is another binary that we need to question. Is it true that all aspects of human experience can be put down to either nature or nurture: either biological or social factors? She points out that each time popular and scientific opinion has swung from nature to nurture or back again it is always homosexuality that is seen as somehow deficient (for example, as being the result of overprotective mothers – nurture – or feminised brains – nature).

Psychologists Peter Hegarty and Felicia Pratto have conducted a range of studies that illustrate this nicely. They found that psychologists and people in general, when asked to explain a difference in sexual orientation or gender, tend to explain it in terms of how gay people differ from straight people, or how women differ from men.

For example, 'women did worse on that task because their brain activity is less focused than men' or 'gay men are more creative because they're more feminine than straight men'.[36] This is a good example of *heteronormativity*.

The search for biological explanations of homosexuality are often justified by saying that if we can prove that people are 'born gay' then gay people will be treated better. Hegarty and Pratto also found that people who believed in biological explanations were no less homophobic than people who accepted more social explanations.[37]

The assumption that biological explanations will somehow legitimise homosexuality also reveals a common slippage that people make when thinking about these issues. They often assume that something being biological makes it somehow more 'real' than something being social: if people are 'born gay' then they can't do anything about it, whereas if it was something that developed over time perhaps they could. There's confusion here between the question of nature vs. nurture and the question of something being determined vs. chosen. The two things don't map onto each other. Saying that something is social, or learnt, is not the same as saying it is chosen (a lifestyle choice or a preference that could easily be otherwise). Take something that is clearly learnt socially – such as wearing clothes. The fact that this is down to nurture rather than nature doesn't mean that it would be easy to strip naked and walk down the street that way!

Biopsychosocial

All of this discussion still risks accepting the premise that things can be divided into nature and nurture, biological and social, and that just isn't the case. As we saw when we explored sex and gender earlier, most aspects of human experiences are actually *biopsychosocial*[38]: a long word which means that they involve our biology, our psychology, and the social world around us, with all of those things influencing each other in complex feedback loops making it impossible to tease apart each element or the direction of any cause-effect relationships.

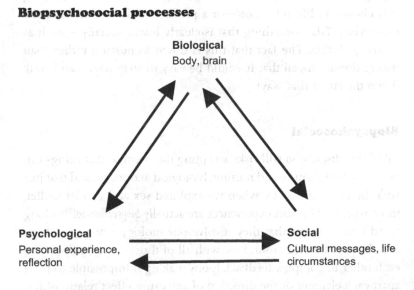

As neuroscientists such as Cordelia Fine have pointed out, the way in which we learn things is undeniably biopsychosocial. For example, if we live in a social world where kids are expected to ride a bike (social) we will likely start trying to do so and, as we learn (psychological), our neural connections will wire up in such a way that we remember how to do it, and our body will start to habitually do what it needs to do to stay upright and move forward (biological). Obviously the connections work in the opposite direction too, in that our existing body and brain abilities and limitations (biological) will make learning to ride a bike more or less easy for us (psychological), which will influence how we experience the (social) world if it is easier or more difficult for us to join our friends on their bikes or to get from A to B. The processes of developing gender roles, or sexual attractions, are probably not so very different to this.

The following diagram and table gives you an (oversimplified) flavour of how some of these influences might work.

Biopsychosocial processes

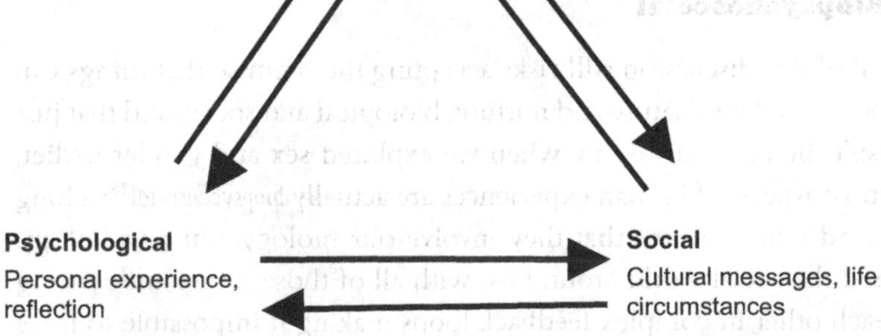

Figure 2.2 Biopsychosocial processes

Going around Figure 2.2 clockwise via the outer arrows, and then counterclockwise via the inner arrows, here are some examples of how each operates, in relation to sexuality.

Table 2.3 Biopsychosocial influences on each other

Direction of influence	**How it can operate**	**Examples**
Biological → social	Our physiological characteristics mean we're treated in certain ways by the world around us	How much our body and brain functions conform to social norms of attractiveness in the time and place we live in.
Social → psychological	This impacts on how we experience the world, and what opportunities are available	If we're regarded as attractive we'll have more potential partners and be treated better generally.
Psychological → biological	Our experiences shape our bodily habits and brain processes	If we're encouraged to be comfortable in our body we'll develop a more relaxed relationship with it – and with sex – than if we're not.
Biological → psychological	Hormonal levels and other features of our biology may point us in certain directions in terms of our desires and characteristics, opening up some experiential possibilities and closing down others	If we're born with the tendency to be more open to new experiences, or more wary, this may gradually develop – through our experiences – into more sexual openness or cautiousness in later life.
Social → biological	Cultural messages embed themselves on our bodies and brains. Social circumstances make certain sexual behaviours possible or impossible	We learn to move in certain ways, or think in certain ways, because of the social expectations, about a person of our gender, race and class, for example. If we spend all our time in an entirely same-sex environment like some prisons and military environments this will influence what sexual opportunities are physically available to us which may shape our sexual behaviours and attractions.

(Continued)

Table 2.3 Continued

Direction of influence	How it can operate	Examples
Psychological → social	We can resist cultural messages and social norms through our actions, potentially opening up different cultural possibilities	Perhaps we get involved in campaigns for sexual rights or sex education which influence the messages that people who come after us receive about sex and sexuality.

It might be helpful to pick one aspect of your own sexuality and work through the diagram considering how the different aspects might be interlinked for you. Again, it's important to emphasise here that something having psychological and/or social elements does not make it any less 'real', 'legitimate', or 'fixed' than it being purely biological – if it is even possible to draw such distinctions given that the way in which our experiences and cultural world write themselves onto our bodies and brains.

As we move through the rest of the book it's particularly important to remember that the way in which our culture views sexuality will influence how available different sexual identities or practices are to us: for example, if we live in a time and place where homosexuality is viewed as a sin, a crime, a sickness, or an acceptable identity. Cultural shifts in how women having sex with women are viewed may partially explain increases in the number of women having same-sex experiences in recent years, for example.[39] And remember the differences the YouGov survey found between people of various generations reporting same-sex attraction (a quarter of all adults, but half of young adults).

CONCLUSIONS

Going back to our summary of assumptions that have often been made in psychology – and in wider culture – about sexuality, let's rethink the list from the start of this chapter:

- Sexuality isn't *binary* (many people are not purely homo- or heterosexual)
- So we can't *categorise* people into one of two boxes on the basis of sexual 'orientation' – it is more like a continuum
- Except actually it's more like multiple continua because there are so many different dimensions to sexuality (beyond what sex/gender we're attracted to – and by the way that isn't binary either) therefore we each have a unique *sexual configuration*
- Sexuality is *fluid* – people experience some aspects of their sexuality as dynamic and changing over time, as well as some as more stable
- Sexuality is *biopsychosocial*: all of these elements combine in complex ways to shape our unique dynamic sexual configuration.

All this clearly has major implications for the questions that we ask in psychology about sexuality, and how we go about answering them. It also has wider implications for how we teach kids about sexuality or how we campaign for sexual and gender equality. Perhaps we need to move away from the 'majority norm – minority other' models towards a model of sexual and gender diversity.[40] Over the next few chapters you'll see how such a model might be a better fit for other aspects of sex too, such as our levels of sexual desire, the sexual practices that we enjoy, and the kinds of sexual relationships we engage in.

3

'PROPER' SEX

As you saw in the last chapter, the psychology of sex has generally focused on sex in the context of sexuality or 'sexual orientation'. This is the sex-related topic often given the most room in psychology textbooks and psychology journals. However, when you considered the question 'What is sex?' in the introduction to this book, sexuality probably wasn't the first thing that sprang to mind. What we tend to mean by sex is 'the sex act', 'having sex', or 'sexual intercourse'.

The areas of psychology that have devoted most attention to this topic are the ones that border on counselling, psychotherapy, and psychiatry; areas such as counselling psychology and clinical psychology where psychologists work therapeutically with clients or patients to alleviate their difficulties. So that's what we'll concentrate on in this chapter, with a particular focus on sex therapy or psychosexual therapy – the kind of therapy that focuses on sexual problems.

Psychology, psychiatry, and psychotherapy have historically categorised sexual problems (or 'disorders') in two main ways: the sexual *dysfunctions* and the *paraphilias*. Sexual dysfunctions are difficulties that get in the way of a person having what is regarded as *functional* sex. Paraphilias are *abnormal* sexual desires. In this chapter we'll focus on functional versus dysfunctional sex to explore what is regarded as the 'proper' sex that people should be having. In the next chapter we'll turn our attention to the normal versus abnormal sex distinction. As always we'll be attending to the ways in which psychology and related disciplines have been involved in *constructing* these functional/ dysfunctional and normal/abnormal distinctions, as well as to what psychological theories and research in this area can tell us about sex.

WHAT IS SEX?

It's useful to start by asking ourselves this question again. Think about it for yourself: if somebody tells you that they've had sex, or that they want to have sex, what do you think they mean?

I feel like I have a fair sense of our wider cultural understanding of sex because I recently spent a lot of time analysing sex manuals and other forms of sex advice for a piece of psychological research.[1] In all I read sixty-five sex advice books – not something I'd necessarily recommend! I also looked at a large number of newspaper problem pages and websites. My colleagues on the project studied sex-related TV documentaries and magazine articles. So between us we got a pretty good idea of how sex advice media understands sex.

We found that what sex advice generally means by sex is penis-in-vagina (PIV) intercourse with the goal of orgasm. On average around 17% of the books I looked at were dedicated to PIV intercourse, compared to 5% on oral sex, 4% on manual sex (using hands), 3% on various forms of kinky sex, 2% on solo sex (or masturbation) and 1% on anal sex. The position of these topics in the books was also telling. By and large things like oral sex, manual sex, and solo sex were covered earlier in the books in sections on 'foreplay', suggesting that they don't count as 'proper sex' in themselves, just as precursors to the 'real thing'. The books covered solo sex almost exclusively as a way of getting better at 'proper sex' by figuring out how you like to be touched or learning how to last longer, for example. Topics such as anal sex, kinky sex, and sex toys were covered later in the books in sections on 'spicing up your sex life'. So again they weren't part of the 'main course' part of the book, but rather additional 'side orders' that some people might want to try.

The point of most of the sex advice books was to help readers to sustain a good sex life throughout a long-term relationship – something that we'll come back to later in the chapter. Again you can see what they meant by sex in the guidance they gave for how to do this. The bulk of the advice focused on varying the positions of PIV sex. Indeed some of the books consisted almost entirely of photographs or diagrams of different ways in which you could have PIV sex. Some books also suggested having PIV sex in different locations, or wearing different clothes, or sometimes adding sex toys or other kinds of sex into PIV sex in order to maximise the chance of both people reaching orgasm. However, PIV intercourse was almost always central.

'So what?' you might be thinking, 'of course sex means PIV intercourse, and of course the point of sex is to get an orgasm'. As with the cultural assumptions about sexuality that we covered in the previous chapter, these things often *seem* obvious because they've come to be so widely taken for granted. Once we start to unpack them, however, we can see how they came to be this way because of the particular historical journey that has brought us to this point. Then we can turn to other psychological theories and research to see some problems with the prevailing view, as well as some ways in which we might usefully take a different approach.

PENISES, VAGINAS, AND ORGASMS

So how did we get to this point: PIV leading to orgasm as the 'gold standard' form of sex which we're all meant to be striving for?

Back to Freud

Again we need to go back to Freud, whose theories of sex – whether we know it or not – have had a marked impact on how we understand sex today.

Before Freud, the early sexologists with their biological focus generally drew on Darwinian thinking and therefore saw the whole purpose of sex as procreation. This explains their desire to categorise and explain any sexual practices and desires that *couldn't* lead to reproduction. What Freud proposed which was so radical at the time was the idea that the purpose of sex was for *pleasure*, not for procreation. He noticed that the bulk of the sex that people had – and wanted – did not have the goal of reproduction. In fact, where procreation is a risk, people often go to great lengths to avoid pregnancy.

Freud's theories didn't completely eradicate the view that 'normal, natural' sex should be that which *could* lead to procreation. You've probably heard that idea expressed yourself – it still haunts many discussions about sexuality. However, his ideas certainly opened up other possibilities. You'll see in the next chapter how recent research has found that humans and other animals have sex for many reasons other than reproducing.

Historians and sociologists of sex suggest that Freud's thinking about pleasure – along with societal changes that were happening at the time – meant that sex became viewed as something like a leisure pursuit: an important element of the married lives of the middle classes. This notion filtered out to society more widely. Then improvements in contraception, particularly the 'sexual revolution' of the pill, took us towards the current view – as expressed in the sex advice books – that sexual satisfaction is a key element of a 'successful relationship'.

The aim of sex

Thinking back to the previous chapter you might remember that Freud proposed that healthy, mature sexuality involved a certain sexual *object* (the 'opposite sex') and a certain sexual *aim*. It is this aim that developed the notion of PIV sex as the gold standard. Basically Freud proposed that all children go through several stages of psychosexual development, theorising that at each stage, the child's libido focuses on a different *erogenous zone* or bodily source of pleasure.

Table 3.1 Freud's stages of psychosexual development

Age	Stage	Normal development
0–1	Oral	Children are preoccupied with their mouths because they feed from the breast. They explore the world orally.
1–3	Anal	Children fixate on their anus. As they become able to control their bowels and bladder, they learn the value of self-control and delayed gratification.
3–6	Phallic	Children become interested in their genitals and begin to masturbate. They notice differences between people's genitals. Unconsciously, they want to possess their opposite-sex parent and are jealous of their same-sex parent (Oedipus complex, see Chapter 2). The conflict is resolved when they learn to identify with their same-sex parent instead of regarding them as a rival.
6–puberty	Latency	Having successfully repressed their libidos, children now go through a period of latency, and they don't experience sexual desire.
Puberty onwards	Genital	Sexual desire re-emerges, focused on the genitals. Women now reach orgasm vaginally instead of clitorally. Sexual activity is partnered rather than solo.

From this table you can see how Freud's theories present PIV sex as the proper, mature form of sexual activity with orgasm as the goal. You can also see how solo sex, as well as oral, anal, and manual sex, are seen as less mature or healthy forms of sex. Like same-sex attraction, lack of sexual desire is regarded as an immature childhood 'phase'. Finally – and importantly – you can see how sexuality became linked to our personalities and identities beyond sex. Freud proposed that some people become *fixated* at earlier stages of psychosexual development, which results in them being a certain kind of person: anally retentive people being obsessive and perfectionist, orally fixated people being naive and immature, and so on.

Even if we may be skeptical of these ideas of early childhood sexuality and unconscious processes in psychology today, they've clearly left their mark on our assumptions about what 'proper sex' should be like, and the place that it should have in people's lives.

Masters of sex

The other people who had perhaps the most marked impact on our current understandings of 'proper sex' are William Masters and Virginia Johnson. You might have seen the TV series *Masters of Sex*, which is based on their lives and work.

William Masters was a gynecologist and Virginia Johnson was his assistant who later became his partner. Like Alfred Kinsey, who we met in the previous chapter, their focus was on the biological and physiological aspects of sex. Unlike Kinsey – and perhaps partly because of the huge controversy which had surrounded Kinsey's research – Masters and Johnson weren't driven to study the diversity of human sexual behaviour. Rather, they focused on discovering how 'normal' sex worked. Later, they turned their focus on how to help people whose sexual experiences didn't follow this pattern to conform to it.

Masters and Johnson also wanted to study the physiology and anatomy of sex directly, rather than just hearing people's *reports* of what they did sexually. For this reason they observed hundreds of people taking part in over 10,000 'cycles of sexual response' under laboratory conditions, while taking measurements of heart rate, blood pressure, etc. They observed PIV sex, masturbation, and 'artificial coition' (masturbation using a dildo-like device which simulated PIV sex while filming it 'from the inside').

The sexual response cycle

The major outcome of Masters and Johnson's research was their four-stage model of sexual response[2]:

1. Excitement: Erectile tissues such as the penis and clitoris become engorged

2. Plateau: The clitoris or testes retract as orgasm approaches
3. Orgasm: There are a series of rhythmical muscular contractions in the vagina and uterus, or penis and urethra. Pulse rate and blood pressure peak, and facial grimacing often occurs.
4. Resolution: Breathing returns to normal and signs of arousal gradually subside. For men this is followed by a refractory period of minutes or hours before arousal can happen again, whereas women do not have such a period and can experience multiple orgasms.

So from Masters and Johnson we get the idea that there is a *sexual response cycle*: a kind of script or set of stages that sex should follow. This includes ideas about how our bodies should respond at each stage, and the 'normal' length of time that each stage should take. You might want to reflect on this yourself: does it match your own experiences of sex if you've had sex? If you were going to divide sex into stages, which ones would you choose? You'll see in a moment that people have had different ideas about this.

Masters and Johnson did dispel some of the myths that were circulating about sex at the time they were writing, and, like Kinsey and his team, their work helpfully got people talking somewhat more openly about sex. For example, they challenged the 'bigger=better' assumption, finding that penis size made very little difference to women's experiences of PIV sex because vaginas are elastic and accommodate themselves to the size of a penis. Also, the size of a flaccid penis isn't a good guide to how large it will be when it is erect because they expand by different amounts.

Importantly, Masters and Johnson also demonstrated that there was no physiological difference between 'vaginal' and 'clitoral' orgasms. If you remember, Freud saw 'vaginal' orgasms as more mature. However, given that the clitoris is actually a large organ which extends back internally through the body, the sensations of orgasm are always produced by the same network of nerves, whether they are stimulated internally or externally or both. Although Masters and Johnson found no difference between these types of orgasm, they didn't manage to let go of the assumption that women *should* be able to orgasm through PIV sex alone, and that being unable to do so was a form of dysfunction.

Shaping the current view of sex

From this quick tour through how understandings of sex have shifted over the last century or so you can again see the role of theories and research in this area in both *informing* us about sex, and in simultaneously *constructing* certain understandings which influence how people will think about – and experience – themselves sexually. For example, a woman who orgasmed only through manual stimulation might – in the late nineteenth century – have seen herself as a sexual deviant (if she could even read the early sexological texts, some of which were written in Latin deliberately so as not to be accessible to uneducated people). In the early twentieth century she might, through psychoanalysis, have come to understand herself as sexually immature and fixated. And in the 1960s she might have been encouraged by Masters and Johnsons' findings, but still have sought to find a way to orgasm from PIV sex – perhaps through the burgeoning field of psychosexual therapy.

Similarly, just think what a radical change solo sex has gone through: from the point over a century ago where there were devices to prevent people from masturbating and it was thought to cause all kinds of physical and psychological problems, to the point now where it is actually prescribed by sex therapists to help people with sexual problems – although masturbating to online pornography has perhaps replaced masturbation in general as the cultural bogeyman (see Chapter 5).

These changes over time demonstrate that our psychological and other scientific knowledge is, at least in part, rooted in the prevailing cultural norms – as well as contributing to them. That means that it could be otherwise. This is an important thought to take forward as we consider how we understand sex psychologically today.

FUNCTIONAL AND DYSFUNCTIONAL SEX?

Masters and Johnson's sexual response cycle was revised slightly by sex therapist Helen Singer Kaplan in the 1970s because it didn't include the feeling of sexual desire that people often experience before they actually become physiologically excited or aroused.[3] Kaplan's cycle included just three stages: desire, arousal, and orgasm. This has become the blueprint for psychiatric, psychological, and psychotherapeutic categories of sexual *dysfunctions*, or *disorders*, since then, most of which involve a person struggling with one of these stages.

The bible for psychiatrists and other kinds of mental health professionals is the American Psychiatric Association's Diagnostic and Statistical Manual (the DSM).[4] This weighty tome lists and describes all of the common 'mental disorders' so that medics and other practitioners can all diagnose people according to the same sets of criteria: the boxes that you have to tick in order to be classified as depressed, anxious, or having a phobia, for example. Outside the US, some bodies also use the World Health Organization's International Statistical Classification of Diseases (ICD), which provides similar lists and generally follows the DSM, with very similar categories and criteria, at least in the area of sex and sexuality. Both the DSM and the ICD include sections on sexual dysfunctions, and sections on paraphilias (which we'll come to in the next chapter).

The sexual dysfunctions

The DSM has been revised every decade or so since the first version in the 1950s and is currently on its fifth edition (DSM-5). The sexual dysfunctions that it lists are based around Kaplan's revision of Masters and Johnson's sexual response cycle. Thus there are categories relating to: lack of desire or sexual interest (*desire*); lack of arousal and 'erectile disorder' (*arousal*); and 'female orgasmic disorder' and 'delayed ejaculation' (*orgasm*). In addition to these there are categories of 'premature (early) ejaculation' and of 'penetration disorder' (struggling to be penetrated due to tension or pain). You might want to think for a moment whether you've ever experienced any of these things yourself. If so, you'll see later that that you share that with at least half of the population.

Looking at these categories gives us a clear idea of what the authors of the DSM consider to be 'functional' as well as 'dysfunctional' sex. Clearly people must go through the full sexual response cycle for functional sex to have occurred. They need to experience sexual *desire*, they need to become *aroused*, and they need to reach *orgasm*. Also PIV sex is obviously an essential feature, given that it is considered to be a disorder if a vagina is not to be able to be penetrated, if a penis can't become erect enough to penetrate, and if ejaculation happens 'prematurely', in other words before penetration has happened.

There's also a tendency, these days, to see sexual 'dysfunctions' as primarily physiological problems which require a medical fix. Masters and Johnson assumed that around 90% of sexual problems had a psychological origin, and only 10% an organic one, whereas recent claims have almost reversed this to 80% organic and 20% psychological.[5] We can see this in the massive popular interest in Viagra and other treatments for erectile dysfunction, as well as the race to find the Holy Grail of a female Viagra which would enhance women's libido. It's intriguing to see that the focus has been on getting men to have erections, and getting women to want sex: this reveals some of our wider cultural assumptions about gender and sex.

In addition to medical treatments, sex therapists also teach patients various physical techniques to address their sexual dysfunctions. These include stopping stimulation at various points for people with premature ejaculation; inserting a series of increasingly large dilators for people whose vaginas are too tense for PIV sex; and sensate focus, where couples who have sexual problems build up gradually from non-genital touching, to genital touching, and eventually PIV.

So what's the problem with this model of sexual function and dysfunction? One useful question to ask yourself about any way of understanding things that you come across in psychology is 'Who does it exclude and who does it include?' and then to consider the implications for both groups of people. You might want to reflect on that question for a moment before reading on.

Exclusions

In terms of who it excludes, the functional/dysfunctional model of sex that we've been looking at definitely assumes that people should have sexual desire, get aroused, and reach orgasm. As we'll see in the next section, although there have been some positive moves in this area, this excludes many asexual people who don't experience sexual attraction.

The model also clearly sees functional sex as sex which involves a penis penetrating a vagina. This excludes all the people whose main sexual activities don't involve this, for example those who prefer solo sex or kinky sex (which we'll look at in the next chapter), as well as couples whose combined sets of genitals are two penises, or two vulvas. If the kinds of sex which are common in same-sex relationships were seen as just as proper or functional as PIV sex, then, along with penetration disorder, we should see categories of sexual dysfunction relating to being unable to control your gag reflex, having a tense anal sphincter, and perhaps repetitive strain injury. There should also be a category for women who orgasm or ejaculate prematurely. Some women do experience problems in orgasming very quickly, but of course this does not interfere with PIV sex so there's no diagnostic category for it.[6]

The risk here is that although the DSM, and sex therapists, don't explicitly say that LGB people aren't having proper sex, that is what is implied by the fact that the categories and treatments relate overwhelmingly to a certain form of heteronormative sex.

Inclusions

The implication that PIV sex is the right, best, or only proper kind of sex is also bad for people who *are* included in this model of sex. Even if you *can* have PIV sex, that doesn't mean that it's the kind of sex that you'll enjoy most. Also it involves far more risk of pregnancy and STIs than many other forms of sex. So it might be helpful if our model of sex included all forms of sex as equally valid, and helped people to experience other kinds of sex in addition to PIV sex.

Feminist psychologists have pointed out some serious gender issues with the functional/dysfunctional model. First, the category of delayed ejaculation for men supports the common assumption that sex is over when the man ejaculates. While women's orgasms are regarded as important, they aren't generally seen as the *essential* component of sex that male ejaculation is, by either sex advice or by sex therapy. You can see how this filters into the everyday experience of the 'orgasm gap'.[7]

We can also see this prioritising of men's sexual experience in the focus on vaginas rather than clitorises in the DSM. The clitoris is the part of the body that is equivalent to the penis and that enables arousal and orgasm. So why do the categories of sexual dysfunction, and measures of arousal such as the vaginal photoplethysmograph that we covered in the last chapter, focus so much on vaginas? Women don't need their vaginas to be penetrated in order to have sexual pleasure, and there are also many other forms of sexual pleasure available to men beyond penetrating a vagina. In fact, research on women's sexuality has found that the majority (70%) of them can't orgasm from PIV alone[8]: they need some kind of external stimulation of their clitoris in addition to – or instead of – vaginal stimulation. So why do we focus so much on PIV sex?

Sex manuals often search desperately for the one sexual position which would stimulate the external clitoris at the same time as allowing PIV: this is often called the CAT or coital alignment technique. However, in all the mainstream sex advice books that I looked at, I never saw the sexual position where a woman lies on top of a man and takes his penis between her legs to rub her clitoris against. This is at least as likely as CAT to be pleasurable for both parties, but of course it doesn't include PIV so it's not considered.

Even the everyday language we have around sex demonstrates the focus on PIV, with men as the active people in sex and women as passive recipients. We talk of 'penetrative' sex, when 'enveloping' sex would be equally valid, and use euphemisms like 'nail' and 'screw'. The multimillion-selling self-help book *Mars and Venus in the Bedroom* explicitly states that women should sometimes lay there 'like a block of wood', and that sex is a natural male need in a way that it isn't for women.[9]

This gendered view of sex is bad for everyone. Obviously it excludes anybody whose gender and/or body doesn't fit the simple male/female binary – as we discussed in the last chapter. It also prevents us from seeing the similarities between, and the variations within, each gender category. For example, there are many similarities in the ways in which our genitals work – because they all began in the same way when we were in the womb. There's also a lot of variety between different people of the same gender about how active or passive they like being sexually, what kind of stimulation they enjoy, and so on.

The 'active initiating man, passive receiving woman' model which we currently have often disempowers women – to the point that many have very little idea what actually turns them on because they're so focused on another person's pleasure rather than their own. The model also pressures men to act as unemotional machines, ever ready for sex, and focused purely on their 'performance'.[10] The idea that soft penises are 'dysfunctional' reinforces these kinds of stereotypes, leading to feelings of failure in men who don't 'measure up', and fear of failure in those who do. It also exacerbates the general cultural pressure on men not to be soft and gentle, or open about their emotions.

All of these expectations make communicating openly about sex very difficult, due to the shame and stigma attached to admitting that the PIV active man/passive woman model of sex doesn't work so well for you. We'll return to what sex therapy might look like if it took a wider perspective on what counted as sex towards the end of the chapter. Meanwhile let's focus a bit more closely on a few of the other underlying assumptions about sex in the current model.

A BASIC HUMAN DRIVE?

One common idea about sex which underlies the model we've been exploring is that sex is necessary or *imperative*. Most sex advice books put forward the view that it's healthy to be sexual, or even that sex is a natural human need akin to eating or breathing. They also claim that sex is vital for relationships: that it's the glue that holds a relationship together, and that having less – or no – sex will inevitably lead to the end of a relationship. Think whether you've heard these ideas yourself and where. Do you agree or disagree that sex is an essential part of being human, and necessary in order for relationships to work?

Historically we can see where these ideas of sex as essential for individuals and for relationships came from. Remember earlier in the chapter when we saw that Freud's theories linked our sexual aim to being a certain kind of person? Our sexual preferences became an inherent feature of our identity according to this model. Also we saw how sex historically became regarded as part of having a successful marriage.

Obviously this *sexual imperative* is useful for selling people books which advise people on how to keep having sex, but is there any validity to it apart from that? Or might it be damaging?

Asexuality

One group of people who have helped to challenge these commonly held assumptions in recent years has been the *asexual* – or ace – communities. Asexual people are people who don't experience sexual attraction. Thanks to online spaces like the Asexuality Visibility and Education Network (AVEN) it has become easier for asexual people to build communities, and for researchers to work with them to find out more about asexuality and to communicate their experiences more widely.

In the past psychologists and psychiatrists assumed that 'lack of sexual attraction' was a sexual dysfunction, and asexual people would have been diagnosed with 'hypoactive sexual desire disorder' or similar. However, psychologist Lori Brotto's work in this area[11] meant that the DSM-5 made it clear that asexual people should not be diagnosed in this way – or treated for any disorder. Research has demonstrated that people don't experience any distress or relationship difficulties due to being asexual: the only difficulty is the stigma that they receive from other people who don't understand asexuality. For example, Mark Carrigan's research with asexual people found that many had been treated in hostile ways by others, often being told that their sexuality was just a phase, that they hadn't met the right person yet, being given sex toys, or even being sexually assaulted by people who said they wanted to 'cure' their asexuality.[12]

Asexuality helps us to see that many aspects of sexual experience are on a continuum, as we saw in the previous chapter in gender of attraction. One of these aspects is the amount of sexual attraction and/or desire that we experience. The common view is that we *should* all conform to some normative amount of sexual desire, having sex a similar 'average' number of times per week. Understanding desire as a continuum, we can acknowledge that some people will experience high levels of sexual feelings, some low, and some none at all. It can be as healthy not to experience sexual desire as to have a libido in any range.

Research on the diversity of asexual experiences is useful for opening our understanding of the different ways in which sexual attraction, desire, and arousal can work. Some asexual people are celibate (don't have sex) and some celibate people are asexual. However, just as there are celibate people who do have sexual desires but choose not to act on them, there are also asexual people who choose to have sex sometimes, even though they don't personally feel desire, for example, in order to give a partner sexual pleasure. Some asexual people are completely averse to sex, some feel more neutral about it. Some *grey-A* and *demisexual* people occasionally experience sexual attraction and see themselves as somewhere on the spectrum from asexual to sexual. For example they might feel sexual but only with one specific person, or enjoy solo sex but not sex with others. As with gender of attraction, some people experience their asexuality as fluid and changeable over time, others as fixed. Many asexual people want romantic or partner relationships, whereas *aromantic* asexual people do not.

The sexual imperative reconsidered

We can see from asexual people's experiences that sex is *not* vital for individuals, or necessary in order to be a healthy person. But what about relationships? Well, clearly many asexual people can and do form happy and healthy relationships without sex. Also, research on sex and relationships more broadly has challenged the common assumption that sex is essential for healthy relationships.

The most recent National UK survey of sexual attitudes and lifestyles (NATSAL) found that, while sex was certainly an important part of a relationship for many people, having less sex or having sexual problems wasn't tied to relationship dissatisfaction, as many sex advisors would have us believe.[13] Similarly, a recent major study on people in long-term relationships found that they had all different levels of sex in their relationships (from none at all to frequent sex) and that this didn't seem to relate to how happy they were with their relationship as a whole or what kind of shape it was in. In fact people often valued other forms of emotional intimacy and/or physical closeness more highly than sex.[14]

We might also usefully challenge the assumptions in a lot of sex advice books that not only is it essential that your relationship is sexual but also that you are in a partner relationship in the first place, that that should be where all your sexual needs get met, and that you should fear losing it. We'll return to some of these ideas in the next chapter when we explore the diversity of ways of having sexual and non-sexual relationships.

THE MEANING OF SEX

We've covered several of the key problems with the current model of sex: it excludes people who aren't heterosexual or into PIV sex;

it offers a limited view of what counts as 'proper sex' and suggests that anybody who can't – or doesn't want to – conform to this is dysfunctional; and it implies that everybody *should* be sexual rather than recognising that sexual desire is on a spectrum and also often fluctuates over the course of people's lives.

Biopsychosocial sex

We also saw earlier that the prevailing view tends to regard sex and its problems as primarily physiological, searching for organic *causes* and medical or physical *fixes*.[15] This tendency to focus on the biological over the psychological and social can be problematic: a biopsychosocial approach is much better at capturing everything that contributes to our sexual experience, whether positive, negative, or a combination of both. Remembering the biopsychosocial approach outlined in the previous chapter, you might want to consider the following examples.

Sex therapist Peggy Kleinplatz describes working with Ms. Smith: a client who was terrified of PIV sex and found that her vagina tensed up any time she attempted it with her fiancé (she might have been diagnosed with 'penetration disorder' or 'vaginismus'). When Kleinplatz explored Ms. Smith's cultural background she found that talking about sex was completely taboo in her family, and sex was viewed as shameful, so she hadn't known what to expect from sexual relationships at all. She had a terrible first relationship with a man who pressured her to let him penetrate her and assaulted her. Talking with Kleinplatz about her experiences in that relationship helped Ms. Smith to share how powerless she felt in relationships, and to explore her anger at what had happened to her. She was able to discuss ways in which she might take control.[16]

I worked with a client, Helen, who was struggling with a problem similar to Ms. Smith's. Helen found it very painful to have PIV sex because her vagina became so tense. Like Kleinplatz I tried to find out about Helen's wider world. We talked a lot about how she felt about her body. She was very negative about it, worrying her partner would be turned off by her 'muffin top' or 'cellulite' and trying to limit herself to sexual positions in which she'd look most attractive. We also talked about the pressures on Helen (as a woman) to always be something for other people: desirable to her partner, a good daughter for her (single) mother, doing all of the emotional labour at work. Our therapy focused on Helen tuning into herself more: learning to value herself and her goals equally to the other people in her life.[17]

These examples illustrate two things: how sexual experiences are biopsychosocial, and how different people have very different meanings around sex.

In both cases we can see how the cultural context the people grew up in was an important part of the picture: for Ms. Smith the shame and taboo around sex, for Helen the importance placed on women being desirable and being all about looking after other people. We can also see how their life experiences combined with cultural messages to give them a particular experience of sex. In Ms. Smith's case her abusive first relationship caused her fear and pain, and in Helen's case her father leaving at a young age left her with a particular fear about losing relationships. These psychosocial elements work on our brains and bodies in the ways described in the last chapter. With women in particular, cultural messages about the need to control their unruly bodies can mean that they get very used to tensing up – fearing the shame, for example, of people knowing they are on their period, or of breaking wind in public.

You can see similar things if you compare case studies of men who lose their erections. Kleinplatz writes about one man who felt he was a failure for having to take Viagra and who was very influenced by that pressure on men to be hard and to perform that I described earlier.[18] The famous therapist Irving Yalom describes a man who had a similar problem, but for him it was much more that sex was a way of soothing himself from the fear of his impending retirement and all the things that he hadn't done in his life. As retirement got closer his old way of distracting himself couldn't keep the anxiety at bay.[19]

So any aspect of sex will have different meanings for different people depending on their cultural context and their individual experiences.

Just think of one sexual experience – an orgasm – and the multiple different ways in which people can experience it. It can be:

> a mechanical release, a demonstration of one's masculine or feminine sexuality, a relief of stress, a loss of control, allowing someone to see you at your most vulnerable, a display of intimacy, the height of physical pleasure, a transcendent spiritual experience, a performance demonstrating prowess, a giving of power to another, an exerting of power over another, a form of creative self-expression, a humorous display of our rather-ridiculous humanity, an unleashing of something wild and animalistic, a deeply embodied experience, an escape from bodily sensations and pain, and/or a moment of complete aliveness or freedom.[20]

We can understand, therefore, why some people might really want orgasms, some might prefer not to, and others might feel more neutral or ambivalent about them.

You might want to think about what sex means to you, or consider different sexual activities and experiences from this perspective. Of course it might well be the case that each one has several different meanings – at different times, or at the same time.

So we've seen how, with all aspects of sex and sexuality, there are aspects of our physiology and the cultural messages that we receive which we *share* with other people, as well as experiences which are *unique* to our particular lives and bodies. For these reasons it's oversimplistic to focus on one universal cause or explanation, or treatment or fix, for any sexual experience or problem. There is no one-size-fits-all form of sex therapy or sex advice. Instead we have to explore each unique person's *lived experience* and the meanings that they have around sex.[21] We'll talk more about these kinds of multiple meanings in the next chapters.

SEX THERAPY

All of this has implications for how sex therapists can best work with clients – and for the kind of psychologically informed sex advice and education that we might want to make available to people. From the last section you've seen that it is important to explore each individual's lived experience of sex rather than assuming everyone has had the same experience of erections, penetration, orgasms, or any other aspect of sex. You've also seen that it's worth remembering that sex is biopsychosocial and giving equal weight to all three aspects (biological, psychological, and social).

Focusing on pleasure rather than goals

Mainstream sex therapy has been criticised for being goal-focused rather than pleasure-focused. Gina Ogden describes it as the 'doing it' theory of sexual normalcy and the 'didja come?' theory of sexual satisfaction![22] There's a risk that focusing on goals will paradoxically have the opposite effect to the one that we want. It's a bit like insomnia: anybody who has suffered with this will know that the worst thing you can do is to try hard to get to sleep. A similar thing is true for trying to get an erection or an orgasm. The more you try to 'achieve' it, the further away it seems to go. Sex therapists are increasingly drawing on mindfulness ideas which encourage people to 'be present' to whatever they are experiencing during sex, instead of trying to make anything particular happen: to focus on the journey rather than any destination.[23] Of course that isn't an easy task, given all the cultural pressure to have PIV sex in multiple positions, and to follow a linear progression from desire through arousal to 'mindblowing' orgasms.

The NATSAL study – which I mentioned earlier – found that 42% of men and 51% of women reported at least one sexual difficulty:[24] that's nearly half of the UK population who regard themselves as having a sexual problem. It's worth wondering how many of those people would see themselves in this way if we didn't have such a limited view of sex: if we expanded out the definition of what counts as sex, as well as making the aim of sex any kind of pleasure rather than reaching a certain goal which is regarded as sexual success.

If the goal of therapy is enabling erections, penetration, and orgasms, we've seen how we can easily miss what sexual problems might be telling us about the wider issues in a person's life. A penis that doesn't want to get erect or a vagina that doesn't want to be penetrated can be seen as potentially sensible: protecting us from revisiting painful experiences, for example, or from treating our bodies like machines.[25]

A focus limited to erections, penetration, and orgasm also misses the possibility of sex therapy doing something much more than re-establishing the capacity for mediocre sex. Peggy Kleinplatz suggests that therapists could usefully offer their clients a range of possibilities. They might choose to do just what works to get them 'functioning', and we should honour that, but if we offer other alternatives alongside this they might choose, for example, to deepen their relationships, to transform their thinking about sex, or to address their lives more widely.[26]

Sex is relational

When we're having sex with another person it's quite likely that it will mean different things to each of us. For example, for the men I mentioned earlier who lost their erections, sex was all about performing or failing, being soothed or feeling anxious. For their partners, sex might have been about getting validation that they were desirable, for example, or may have served as a regular ritual which made them feel secure in their relationship. So having sexual problems or stopping having sex would have different meanings for each person involved. Without that *relational* understanding we might assume that sex will mean the same thing to the other person as it does for us, or we might put extra pressure on the situation – by assuming, for example, that they will want a certain kind of sex, or by trying to persuade them because of what we want out of it. If somebody is in a relationship then it's useful to include everybody concerned in therapy because it is something that's happening between them, not in isolation.

Another myth about sex which is perpetuated by mainstream sex advice is that partners should match perfectly in terms of both the amount of sex that they want, and the kind of sex they want. That's actually hardly ever the case. In any relationship there'll likely be a certain amount of overlap in extent and types of desires, and also areas where there's no overlap at all. Also, because amount and type of desire fluctuate over time, this will shift and change over the course of the relationship.[27]

If we could expand our understandings of sex then it could be more possible for partners to acknowledge that these kinds of discrepancies and fluctuations are normal, and they could talk about the various options for meeting diverse sexual desires through solo sex, fantasy, or other sexual relationships, for example. However, psychologist Sandra Byers has found that levels of open communication about sex in relationships is very low. People who had been in relationships for over a decade still hadn't told their partners all of their sexual likes and dislikes: They understood about 60% of what their partner liked sexually but only around 20% of what they didn't like.[28]

You might find it helpful to consider, if you have sex, how many of your sexual tastes you share with the people you have sex with. The cultural pressures and shame around sex have major implications for ensuring that sex is consensual, something we'll turn to in the next chapter.

CONCLUSION

You've seen in this chapter that psychology, psychiatry, and sex therapy have tended to see 'proper' sex as PIV intercourse leading to orgasm. People who don't experience desire, arousal/erections, or orgasms have been regarded as dysfunctional or disordered.

We've explored how this limited view of sex is present in wider culture, and excludes many people, as well as placing unrealistic pressures and restrictions on those it does include. Jenny Van Hoof has found that young couples are definitely influenced by these limited understandings of sex, tending to see sex as an essential feature of long-term relationships, assuming that men need sex, and that keeping a good sexual relationship going is women's work.[29]

A more open and expansive version of sex, based on the kind of research and theories we've covered in this chapter, might look something like this:

- Acknowledging that it's perfectly healthy to have any level of sexual desire (from none to high and everything in between) and for this to stay the same, or change, through your life and relationships.
- Recognising that all forms of consensual sex are equally valid, including solo sex and sex that involves rubbing hands or bodies together as well as various forms of penetration.
- Realising that sex has different meanings for different people and tuning into our own biopsychosocial experience of sex, and that of the people we're sexual with.
- Making the focus of sex 'being present' to how it feels, for everyone involved, rather than reaching any particular goal.

As with the last chapter, an important message here is that sex is diverse. Instead of trying to compare everybody against some assumed norm, we could embrace the diversity of levels and types of desire that people have. This is something that we'll go on to explore in more depth in the next two chapters.

4

'NORMAL' SEX

In the previous chapter we considered the implications of dividing sex into functional and dysfunctional forms. In this chapter we'll explore the other way that sex has commonly been divided up: into normal and abnormal kinds of sex. Remember that in the current psychiatric diagnoses and in psychology textbooks, these are the two main categories of sexual disorders: the sexual *dysfunctions*, and the *paraphilias* (or abnormal sexual desires).

You saw in Chapter 2 that, since the outset of psychological thinking about sex, a key project of psychologists and other scholars in this area has been to separate normal from abnormal sex. From the early sexologists to the current American Psychiatric Association's Diagnostic and Statistical Manual of Mental Disorders (DSM-5) we see lists of sexual deviations, perversions, or paraphilias. But what do we mean by normal and abnormal in this context? And is this a useful way to divide up different kinds of sex?

CONCERNING SEX

Before we go any further, it's useful to think for yourself about how you would distinguish different sexual practices. The following exercise is one that I developed to use when I train therapists and other practitioners on the *paraphilic disorders*, as they are currently termed.[1]

As you read down the list, ask yourself whether or not you'd be concerned if a friend revealed that they'd taken part in this activity. When you reach the end of the list, ask yourself which ones you found the most and least concerning, and why. You might find it useful to note down any key concepts that you find yourself using to distinguish the concerning ones from the less concerning ones.

- An individual gets a rush out of being put in terrifying situations that make him scream and cry out in fear. He engages other people to put him in a special device which will result in these effects. When his time in the device is up, his face is white and he has tears in his eyes, but he begs them to let him go through it again.
- A woman asks strangers to cause her extreme pain to her genital area. She does this regularly, as she feels more attractive following the painful session. Sometimes, she'll even do it to herself. If it's done right, no permanent harm results.
- A small group of people arrange to meet in a private space in order to watch others role-playing being raped, humiliated, and tortured. They find this an enjoyable way of spending their evening.
- Two people arrange to take part in a public scene. They spend a great deal of time preparing separately in advance. On the night they dress for the occasion in clothes made of satin. Watched by a gathered group of people, they strike each other. The scene is considered successful if one of them briefly loses consciousness. The beatings are so severe they can result in permanent damage.
- A woman spends several hours preparing her appearance. She chooses from items of clothing on which she has spent several thousand pounds, all of which painfully restrict parts of her body, forcing it into an unnatural shape and making it impossible for her to function normally. Over an extended period of time she

knows this will damage her permanently. However, she experiences great pleasure despite the pain.

- As part of a group ritual a man consents to an event which he knows will be gruelling, although he doesn't know exactly what will take place. During the event, among other things, he is put in an altered state of consciousness, stripped, and left alone in public.
- An individual gives his life over to his master. He won't do anything that is disapproved of under the code of rules his master has set. He won't allow himself to experience sexual satisfaction until he has undergone the procedures his master sets out as necessary, although he often finds himself in a state of arousal and wishes he could. He mostly spends time with other people who have also pledged themselves to the same master, although none of them have ever met him in person.

DRAWING THE LINE

When I use this exercise in training it generally leads into a useful discussion about the kinds of lines that we draw to delineate concerning from non-concerning, and acceptable from unacceptable, sexual practices.

Some people say that the dividing line, for them, is about whether the practice causes *damage* and whether that damage is *permanent* or *temporary*. Others distinguish between harm caused to *oneself* or to *another person*. Some say that it makes a difference how *rare* or *common* an activity is, or how *extreme* it seems to be. For some the *number of people* involved plays a part in their feelings about the activity, as does whether it is in the context of an *existing relationship* or with a *stranger*. People speak about lines around *illegal* activities, and also around *fantasy* vs. *reality*. Others mention whether activities cause *distress* or *pleasure*.

People also frequently mention drawing lines based on whether activities are *consented* to by the people involved: whether people freely chose to get involved and whether they could give *informed consent*. For example, the group ritual often causes concern because the participant doesn't know what he's consenting to and members of the public may not have consented to witnessing it.

Another similar activity that you could usefully try is to list all of the sexual practices that you're aware of and then try to put them on a continuum from most acceptable to least acceptable. Draw a line on the continuum at where you think the division is between acceptable sex and unacceptable sex. That might give you some further clues about the criteria that you yourself use to delineate sex. You might also consider where you think your current understanding came from.[2]

Keep hold of your own thoughts on the exercise because we'll come back to it over the course of this chapter. You'll see that psychologists, psychiatrists, and psychotherapists have also tended to use a mixture of these different concepts to decide what count as paraphilic disorders: harm, commonality, relationship context, legality, fantasy/reality, choice, and consent.

NORMAL AND ABNORMAL SEX?

Let's look now at the most recent list of paraphilic disorders, as defined by the DSM-5.

The paraphilic disorders

The DSM-5 defines paraphilias as sexual practices that involve 'intense and persistent sexual interest other than . . . in genital stimulation or preparatory fondling with phenotypically normal, physically mature, consenting human partners'. This is the current list of the paraphilic disorders with a brief explanation of what each means:[3]

- Voyeuristic disorder (sexually enjoying watching other people)
- Exhibitionistic disorder (enjoying being watched)
- Sexual masochism disorder (finding it exciting to be humiliated, tied up, and/or to receive painful stimulation)

- Sexual sadism disorder (finding it exciting to do those kinds of things to another person)
- Fetishistic disorder (getting turned on by objects or materials)
- Transvestic disorder (becoming aroused by wearing clothes usually associated with the 'opposite sex')
- Frotteurietic disorder (getting turned on by rubbing up against other people)
- Pedophilic disorder (being sexually attracted to children)

So you can see that several of the examples in our exercise earlier combine elements of these, particularly the first five. You might want to consider which – if any – of these might apply to you to some degree.

Up until the last edition of the DSM, simply having these sexual interests was enough to class you as being paraphilic and therefore as having a mental disorder. However, for the DSM-5 they changed this so that the interest alone did not imply a disorder. In order to be diagnosed as having a paraphilic *disorder*, you now have to meet a second criterion (criterion B) whereby it causes you some distress. This is how it is worded for sexual sadism disorder, for example (the others are very similar).

> Criterion A. Over a period of at least 6 months, recurrent and intense sexual arousal from the physical or psychological suffering of another person, as manifested by fantasies, urges, or behaviours.
>
> Criterion B. The individual has acted on these sexual urges with a non-consenting person, or the sexual urges or fantasies cause clinically significant distress or impairment in social, occupational, or other important areas of functioning.

So if you occasionally find one or more of the things listed above to be sexually exciting, you wouldn't meet criterion A or B. If it was an intense and ongoing source of excitement which you were quite happy with, then you'd meet criterion A, but still not be classed as having a disorder. If you had also acted on it non-consensually, or it caused distress or impairment, then you'd have a paraphilic disorder, according to the DSM.

Before we go on to consider some problems with the paraphilic disorders, reflect for yourself on whether you agree that somebody who met these criteria should be classed as having a mental disorder.

Criticisms of the paraphilias

Starting with the overall definition of paraphilic disorders in the DSM, as with sexual dysfunctions in the previous chapter you can see that through defining abnormal and dysfunctional sex, the DSM also defines what is normal or functional sex. In this case it is genital stimulation with somebody who is normal in terms of their observable physical or biological characteristics. So again, solo sex and mutual masturbation aren't regarded as normal sex, and neither is sex with (presumably) intersex people, trans people, and possibly disabled people or people with larger or smaller body sizes than the norm (depending on how far you take the definition of 'phenotypically normal').[4] These aspects of the DSM definitions are problematic for all the reasons we considered in Chapter 3.

Perhaps the most compelling criticism that people have made about the paraphilias is that they are simply a reflection of our current social mores rather than any kind of objective scientific list of pathological sexual practices.[5] This is underlined when you consider the fact that homosexuality was classed as a mental disorder in the DSM until 1973, and in the World Health Organization's International Classification of Diseases (ICD) until 1992. If same-sex attraction was once a disorder and now isn't, might the other paraphilias simply be reflections of what wider culture thinks is acceptable and unacceptable sexually?

Here it's useful to return to the exercise we did before. As you went down the list, you may well have realised that there is another element to this exercise, along with it being a useful way into considering the lines we draw around sexual activities. All of the activities listed are actually commonplace in mainstream culture. They describe, in order: a fairground ride, a bikini wax, watching a horror movie like *Hostel* or *Saw*, a boxing match, wearing high-heeled shoes or a corset, a stag do or bachelor party, and the practices of many religious people.

This aspect of the exercise highlights how much *more* difficulty people tend to have with activities that are culturally non-normative or stigmatised than those that are culturally accepted. Once the 'real' activities are revealed, people often start to ask themselves whether they were *really* so bothered about damage, distress, or consent given that they suddenly find that their concern disappears when they know what the activities actually are. Other useful comparisons to make would be play piercing in a kink context versus acupuncture or tattooing; and suspension bondage versus rock climbing.

The history of homosexuality in the DSM helps to reveal a further issue with the paraphilias. When homosexuality was first removed from the DSM it was replaced with the category of 'ego-dystonic homosexuality', which basically meant people having same-sex desires that they were distressed by or which caused impairment to their lives: rather like the recent move from 'paraphilias' to 'paraphilic disorders'. The problem with this, of course, is that when you have a sexual identity or practice which is viewed as unacceptable in wider culture – to the point at which it was recently considered to be a mental disorder – you're not likely to feel 100% brilliant about it! Those people who are disturbed by their kinky sexual desires – or who previously were by their same-sex desires – may well not be disordered in any inherent sense, but just struggling to exist in a culture that sees them as sick, bad, or unacceptable. Of course continuing to list certain sexual practices in the DSM, even with the caveat that they're only disorders if people are unhappy with them, only perpetuates the stigma.

Finally, Charles Moser and many others have criticised the paraphilias for being muddled, unclear, inconsistent, and lacking in any basis in evidence.[6] If you think back to the reasons people gave for delineating sexual practices earlier, a mixture of these are in play in the DSM diagnoses. Some are there because they are inevitably non-consensual if acted upon (e.g. pedophilic disorder) or often non-consensually acted upon (e.g. frotteurietic and voyeuristic disorders). With others the concern seems to be more about potential harm to others (e.g. sexual sadism disorder) or self (e.g. sexual masochism disorder). And with others, the only conceivable problem would be that the person themselves or people in their lives had problems with it (e.g. fetishistic and transvestic disorders). As we'll go on to see, many of the so-called paraphilias are actually very common, few are linked to mental distress in the general population, and all except pedophilia *can* be acted upon in consensual ways.

In addition to the slippage between different reasons for classifying something as paraphilic (consent, commonality, harm, etc.) there is the issue of line-drawing. You may well have thought yourself that at one end of the spectrum many of the paraphilias apply to a whole lot of people. Think about how many folks enjoy watching sex-themed movies (a form of voyeurism), or wearing certain materials in sexy outfits (animal print or lace, for example – a form of fetishism), or enjoy turning people's heads when they walk into the room (a form of exhibitionism).

At what point do we decide that a person has strayed too far towards the 'abnormal' end of the spectrum? What do we mean by abnormal? And is 'normality to abnormality' the best spectrum to be using in the first place? As Moser provocatively points out, we could class heterosexual attraction as a paraphilic disorder just as much as any other sexual practice: it often involves recurrent and intense arousal which is acted on non-consensually or does cause significant distress and impairment.[7]

Learning from the margins

Until recently, psychologists and related professionals who studied the paraphilias, or 'abnormal' sexual practices, have focused on *explaining* why people might engage with them: often trying to come up with universal causes of sadism, masochism, etc. in a way similar to the way they did with same-sex attraction (see Chapter 1). In recent years, however, many of us have questioned that way of thinking, rooted as it is in cultural assumptions about acceptability, and dubious notions that any human behaviour can have one explanation that applies to everybody who engages in it (see Chapter 2).

Recent scholars and professionals have taken the radically different approach of asking what we might *learn* from those at the outer limits of human sexual experience which could be of use to everybody, rather than how we might explain them and keep them at a comfortable distance.[8] In the next two sections we'll look at what we now know about kink, and about non-monogamous relationships, from this kind of psychology, and the light that this shines on sexual practices and sexual relationships more widely.

KINK ETC.

Kink and BDSM are umbrella terms which are more frequently used for what the DSM called sadism and masochism. Often the terms are used loosely enough that a lot of exhibitionism, voyeurism, and fetishism could fall under those umbrellas as well. BDSM stands for bondage and discipline, dominance and submission, and sadomasochism, so it covers a pretty wide range of practices.

Is BDSM a paraphilia?

Paraphilias are commonly defined as *conditions* characterized by *abnormal sexual* desires, typically involving *extreme or dangerous* activities, so let's start by examining whether BDSM can meet these criteria.

First, in order for kink to be a *condition or disorder* we'd expect kinksters to have higher rates of psychological problems than other people. Early research in this area did find relationships between being into BDSM and various forms of mental distress – until people pointed out that most of that research consisted of mental health professionals writing about their clients! This is an example of the *clinician illusion* whereby practitioners assume that a practice or identity is pathological because the only people they've seen with it in their clinic have been struggling. Of course pretty much all the people who clinicians see are struggling, so that's pretty meaningless.

From the 1980s onwards psychologists and other researchers have started studying kinksters in the general population and comparing them against people who aren't into BDSM, on various measures. This kind of research has found no evidence that kinky people are any more psychologically unhealthy than anyone else.[9] In fact the most recent research suggests that they may even be *more* healthy,[10] with one study finding that BDSM practitioners were, on average, less neurotic, more extraverted, more open to new experiences, more conscientious, less sensitive to rejection, and reported greater well-being than a control group. Another study found no evidence for the common idea that kinky inclinations are rooted in childhood abuse and trauma, as suggested in movies like *Secretary* and *Fifty Shades of Grey*. The research found that kinksters have childhoods that are indistinguishable from those of other people.[11]

What about being *abnormal*? Research suggests otherwise. Around two-thirds of people have fantasies about bondage, and other common interests such as spanking and roleplay are not far behind.[12] Over a third of people – in the US at least – use masks, blindfolds, and bondage equipment during sex.[13] BDSM equipment is sold in high street sex shops, and – of course – the *Fifty Shades of Grey* books and films have been international bestsellers, suggesting that some degree of interest in kinky sex is commonplace: a majority rather than minority interest.

Paraphilias are about *sexual* desires, but is BDSM always sexual? For some people BDSM is about sex and for some there are orgasms involved. For other people there might be a different kind of climax (of sensation or emotion, for example), or no climax at all.[14] For some, BDSM is actually something more like a leisure activity, a sport, an art form, or a spiritual practice, than what we tend to think of as sex.[15]

Finally, is BDSM *extreme* or *dangerous*? This is still a common depiction in mainstream media where the cops chasing down the serial killer go looking for him in the BDSM club, or the person getting into kink ends up on a slippery slope to more and more extreme activities.

Many psychologists and therapists still believe these stereotypes and try to stop people from engaging in kink.[16] Actually, again, kinksters are no more likely to be abusive than anybody else. Of course, that means that there will be folk in the BDSM world who will be abusive (just as there are in the general population). But it's important to remember it is no *more* likely there.

Kinksters also don't turn up in the emergency room any more than anybody else.[17] In fact, many of the activities that were mentioned in the exercise at the start of this chapter are far more risky and non-consensual than the many of the most common kink activities (spanking and bondage, for example). And there is no slippery slope: most people experience 'levelling off' after their initial BDSM experiences.[18] Of course some kinksters do engage in what might be considered to be more extreme practices – making kink a large part of their lives, for example, or seeking to endure high levels of pain or stimulation. However, this can be regarded as analogous with long-distance runners, rock-climbers, or other sports people. They also devote a lot of their lives to activities which can be very painful or risky because they are excited by what they are doing or committed to enduring it.

So we've seen that none of the things that make something a paraphilia apply to BDSM as a whole. It's not associated with psychological problems, it's not abnormal, it's not necessarily even always sexual, and it's no more extreme or dangerous than many culturally accepted human behaviours. So what about turning the question around and asking what everyone else might stand to learn from kinksters?

Learning from the kinksters

People who are unfamiliar with BDSM often assume that it involves a small range of things and that everyone does it for the same reason. There is a common stereotype, for example, of high-powered businessmen going to a leather-clad dominatrix to be whipped. Psychologists in the past also tried to come up with single explanations to explain all sadism or all masochism, such as it being an escape from having to be in control, as in this example. Actually BDSM includes many different practices and people do it for a multiplicity of different reasons.

For example, BDSM can include: physical sensations (from feathers to candlewax to floggers), bondage (from handcuffs to rope to intricate ribbons), domination and submission (e.g. somebody waiting on somebody else, somebody ordering another person around), discipline (e.g. spanking, telling off), dressing up, and role-play (cops, pirates, medical, school, etc.). And all these things can happen separately or in combination.

For some people BDSM *can* be a way of giving up control and letting go, for others it is a fun, playful activity. It can mean taking on a different role and being somebody else for a while, it can be a form of relaxation, or it can be a way of showing strength and how much you are capable of enduring. It can help some people to explore something that scares them (such as pain or bullying), it can be a way of building intimacy with another person, or it can provide a reason for being looked after and cared for afterwards. It could mean many of these things even for the same person, or on different occasions.[19]

So BDSM practices can point to ways in which we might expand our erotic imaginations beyond what we've learnt to regard as 'proper sex' (see Chapter 2) so that we might explore different parts of the body, different sensations, different psychological states, and different relationship dynamics, that we could enjoy or find exciting. BDSM can also help us to remember how every activity will have different meanings for different people. For example, someone can enjoy spanking 'because they like to feel humiliated, because they like the physical sensation, because they like seeing how much they can take, because they like giving up control to another person, because it makes them feel like a child, because it feels taboo, because their buttocks are a major erogenous zone for them, because it feels like an act of great intimacy with a partner, and for many other reasons, or combinations of reasons'.[20]

Kinksters have come up with many useful ways of tuning into what they might enjoy, and communicating this to others. This is particularly helpful given what we learnt in the last chapter about how poorly people tend to communicate with sexual partners about sex. For example, 'yes, no, maybe' inventories help people to consider a wider range of sexual activities and whether they would like to try them. Traffic-light safewords or scales of 1 to 10 help people to check in with each other during activities about how much they're enjoying it.[21]

However, perhaps the most useful contribution from kink communities in recent years has been their increasingly sophisticated thinking on sexual consent. We'll return to this in depth towards the end of this chapter.

NON/MONOGAMIES

One aspect of what is usually considered 'normal' sex which isn't explicitly mentioned in the list of paraphilic disorders is monogamy. Like the *sexual imperative*, which we covered in Chapter 2 and *heteronormativity*, which we covered in Chapter 1, the idea that it's normal to be monogamous – or *mononormativity* – is taken so for granted that people rarely feel the need to mention it. However, it is ever-present as a background assumption both in psychology and in wider culture.

Mononormativity

When I reviewed psychology textbooks I found that all the theories and research they included on relationships assumed that these would be monogamous. Non-monogamy was only ever covered in the context of affairs or infidelity, which was represented as dangerous for relationships.[22] Relationship therapy has historically assumed the same thing: viewing married or long-term coupledom as the normal way of having relationships and trying to prevent people from acting on any attractions outside of this. Sex advice books acknowledge that it is extremely common to fantasize about sex with people other than your partner, and about group sex, but warn against ever acting on these desires as they will inevitably result in jealousy and break-up. One of the most entertaining ways in which they address this paradox is to suggest that a couple having sex in front of a mirror is equivalent to having a threesome![23] Of course much mainstream media relies on *mononormativity*. How many of the plotlines in Hollywood movies, soap operas, and tabloid scandals would make sense if it was accepted that people could love – and/or have sex with – more than one person?

However, this idea that monogamy is the only way of doing relationships is deeply problematic. It is *ethnocentric*: assuming that western ideals represent the right and normal way of doing things. Globally far more societies operate on some form of non-monogamy than on monogamy.[24] Even within western cultures the norm of monogamy obscures a reality in which secret non-monogamy is at least as common as monogamy, with rates of hidden infidelity in marriage as high as 50 or 60%.[25] This means that we're in the position where many people are unable to have their ways of structuring their relationships legally recognised, and many others feel shame and guilt, insecurity and jealousy, in relationships which they have to pretend are monogamous when actually they are not.

Open non-monogamy

The last decade or two has seen an explosion of interest in various forms of open or consensual non-monogamy. As with asexuality, the increased potential for finding information, community, and partners online has been a large part of this increase.

When I started studying this area in the early 2000s, there were small but growing communities of swingers, gay men in open relationships, and polyamorous people.[26] The former two groups generally form couple relationships but have sex, alone or together, with people outside those relationships. Polyamory, on the other hand, involves having multiple love relationships in various forms. Psychologist Terri Conley estimates that around 5% of people in the US now engage in some form of consensual non-monogamy,[27] and the figures are probably similar in other western countries.

As with kink, when some psychologists finally shifted from simply assuming that open non-monogamy was pathological or dangerous, their initial focus was on checking out and challenging many of the stigmatising stereotypes about non-monogamous people.[28] Terri Conley and her colleagues found that people generally think that a life-long monogamous relationship is most beneficial for a couple's sex life, happiness, and well-being, and for any children they have.[29] However, there's evidence which challenges all of these beliefs and suggests that forms of open non-monogamy can be equally beneficial. In addition to avoiding the stress involved in the deception of secret non-monogamy, researchers like Elizabeth Sheff and Maria Pallotta-Chiarolli have found many benefits of open non-monogamy for children, including the extra emotional and practical resources of having multiple parents, and role models who emphasise open communication.[30] In common with many monogamous relationships, pitfalls include the problems of attachment following breakup, and there is also the problem of stigma due to being part of a non-monogamous family in a mononormative world.[31]

Learning from open non-monogamy

As with kinky, asexual, and LGBT people, it can be useful to reverse the usual trend of psychologists searching for explanations for these marginalised identities and practices, and instead asking what everyone might learn from the margins.

Open non-monogamous relationships have raised some important questions about the ideal form of monogamous partnership that is our current cultural norm. For example, historians and sociologists in this area have pointed out that this kind of coupledom – and the nuclear family – are relatively new phenomena.[32] In the past, people frequently entered into relationships for reasons to do with family, money, work, childcare, and so on rather than for romantic love (although that doesn't mean that romantic love was never involved). In the current version there's a lot of pressure on partners to be everything to each other: best friend, lover, and co-parent; providing belonging, excitement, validation, security, and helping us meet our goals in life. Psychologist Bjarne M. Holmes has linked believing strongly in The One perfect partner to having worse relationships,[33] and psychotherapist Esther Perel has written about how difficult it is for relationships to provide warmth and stability at the same time as passion and excitement.[34]

None of this means that open non-monogamy is necessarily a *better* way of having relationships than monogamy. Indeed, several authors have written about the ways in which open non-monogamy can be just as problematic as monogamy, with communities often excluding anyone outside a white middle-class norm,[35] and perpetuating rules and gender roles which can be just as restrictive as those in monogamous relationships.[36] Instead of buying into a new binary (monogamy vs. non-monogamy) and trying to figure out which one is better, it can be more useful to recognise the diversity of ways of doing relationships that are available and equally valid.

This is why I titled this section non/monogamy. Increasingly the dividing lines in this area are becoming blurred. For example, we might wonder where to situate monogamish relationships (which are somewhat open), hook-up cultures,[37] friends-with-benefits arrangements, or soft swinging (where couples don't go as far as having sex with other people). We also need to recognise the range of different ways of being openly or secretly non-monogamous, from 'don't ask, don't tell' arrangements, to various forms of hierarchical non-monogamy (having primary and secondary partners), egalitarian polyamory (having multiple partners on the same level, for example in a triad or family), and solo poly (being an independent individual with more than one partner).[38]

As we saw with sexual attraction and desire in previous chapters, monogamy might also be more usefully viewed on a continuum from exclusive to open, with some people moving around that continuum over the course of their lives and others remaining relatively fixed.[39] You might find it useful to imagine where you would put yourself on such a continuum. If we view relationship styles as diverse rather than on some right/wrong, normal/abnormal binary then people stand more chance of being able to find an approach which works for them.

The communication which is prioritised in many forms of open non-monogamy[40] can also be helpful to people in all kinds of relationships. People in monogamous relationships often assume that they share understandings of what monogamy means, but frequently they eventually find out that they differ, and this can often cause a crisis.[41] It's very common for one person to think that looking at pornography or having cybersex is okay while the other person thinks this is cheating, or for there to be disagreements around remaining friends with ex-partners. The idea of having open conversations about the kind of contracts and disclosures that we want or don't want in relationships can be helpful for everyone.[42]

Recent work in this area is taking the ideas from open non-monogamy further, asking profound questions about how we delineate different kinds of relationships. For example, many forms of monogamy and non-monogamy still prioritise romantic relationships over friendships and other kinds of relationships. Some prioritise primary over secondary partners, or romantic partners over sexual ones, or recent forms of polyamory over traditional forms of polygamy. Relationship anarchy challenges such different valuing of relationships, and solo poly raises important questions about how singledom is culturally stigmatised.[43]

Scholars are beginning to link questions about how we value people differently in interpersonal relationships to wider current issues about the different value placed on different lives. This includes questions around immigration and refugees; austerity measures, class, and disability; racism, Islamophobia, and the #BlackLivesMatter campaigns; the treatment of trans people and sex workers,[44] and our relationships with other species and with the planet.[45]

BEYOND THE SEX HIERARCHY

Hopefully this discussion of the paraphilias in general, and kink and non-monogamy in particular, has got you thinking critically about the whole agenda of creating sex hierarchies. We've seen throughout this book how people cannot simply be divided into majority and minority sexualities, functional or dysfunctional sexual experiences, or normal or abnormal sexual desires, and how attempts to do so are bad both for those who are put in the inferior category *and* those who are put in the superior one.

The charmed circle

In the 1980s the sociologist Gayle Rubin presented the following diagram to illustrate the sex hierarchy that is so often perpetuated by psychology, medicine, laws, religions, and mass media.[46]

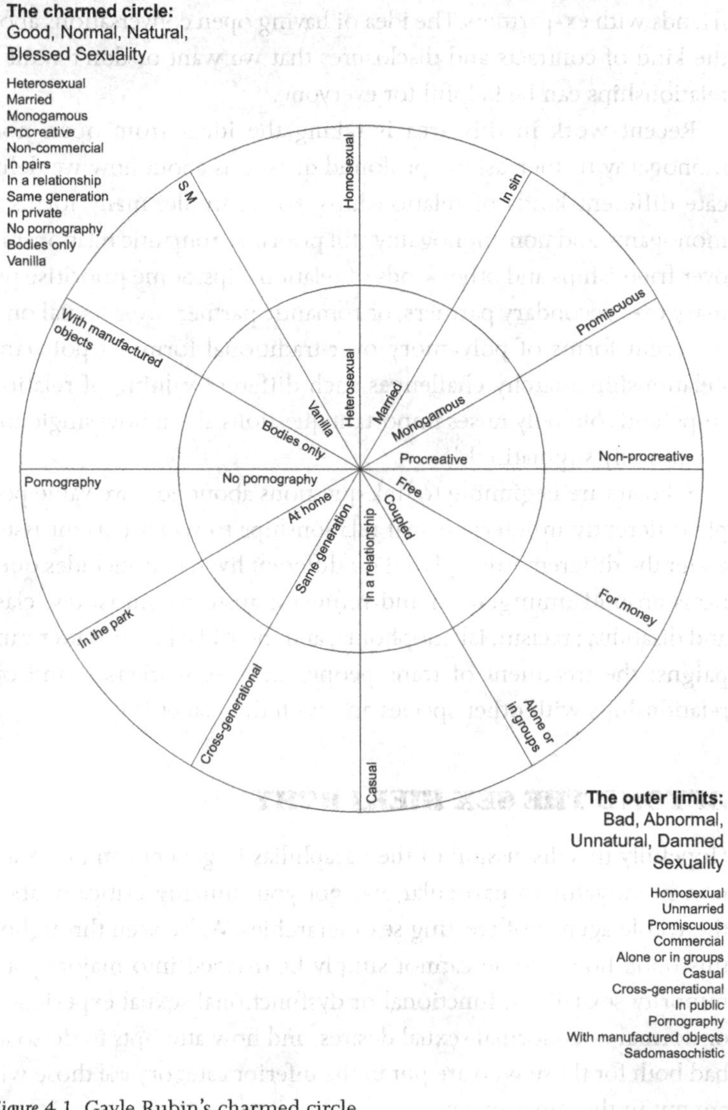

Figure 4.1 Gayle Rubin's charmed circle

In the inside circle of the diagram we have what she called the 'charmed circle' of sexuality. The more people's sexual relationships and practices fall into this circle, the more acceptable, good, normal, and natural they are seen as being. In the outside circle of the diagram we have the 'outer limits' of sexuality. The more people's sexual relationships and practices fall into this circle, the more unacceptable, bad, abnormal, and unnatural they are viewed as being. It is a matter of degree. Consider a heterosexual woman who has casual sex, then add in taking payment and filming herself. Or think about the recent same-sex marriage debates. How did gay people represent themselves in terms of these circles?

Linked to the idea of a sex hierarchy is the fear that a person might fall into unacceptable sex. Rubin says that we tend to see it as a slippery slope: if someone strays outside of the charmed circle a little bit they might get sucked all the way out of it. She says that we fear that if we step outside 'the barrier against scary sex will crumble and something unspeakable will skitter across'. Part of the purpose of categories such as the paraphilias is to police this boundary, but it is difficult because it's built on shifting cultural sand: as you'll see in the next chapter, increasing pressure to have sex that is 'great' as well as 'normal' means that many people are walking a tightrope trying to be both normal enough and sexy enough.[47]

You might want to think back to the answers you gave about where you would draw the line between acceptable and unacceptable – or concerning and non-concerning – sex at the start of the chapter. To what extent do these map onto the kind of sex hierarchy Rubin speaks about?

Before we think about alternative approaches to sex hierarchies and line drawing, let's go on a quick tangent to consider the idea of 'natural' sex. You can see from Rubin's diagram that ideal or acceptable forms of sex are often conflated with those which are natural.

What is natural sex?

It's often assumed that animals only have sex for procreation – in order to pass on their genes – and that this means that, whatever we want to say about sexual diversity in humans, 'natural' sex is males and females having penis-in-vagina intercourse. This isn't the case, however.

In fact, having sex at all is a recent phenomenon. Sexual reproduction in animals only began 300 million years ago and asexual reproduction is still the norm in many animals and plants, probably because it requires a lot less time and energy than sexual reproduction, and there is no risk of not finding a mate.[48] Many species who do sexually reproduce – particularly fish – also change sex during their lifetimes.[49]

It also seems that other meanings of sex are at least as important as reproduction across animal species. Sex can serve to strengthen bonds between animals and within a group.[50] Many animals masturbate, and many female animals engage in sex when they're pregnant or use forms of birth control. Trans-species sex also happens, which can't result in procreation.[51] Same-sex sex happens in over 450 different species of animals across the globe, in every major animal group of all sexes, sometimes to the extent that it surpasses heterosexual behaviour in that species.[52] More than half of mammal and bird species engage in bisexual activities.

Very few animal species are monogamous, or pair-bond for life,[53] so it could be argued that non-monogamy is more natural than monogamy. This demonstrates how spurious 'natural' arguments are, despite how often people deploy them to support normative assumptions and how rarely they mention them when they support non-normative ones.

Alternatives to the sex hierarchy

Authors such as Gayle Rubin and Chess Denman[54] argue that if we could get away from the desire to divide sexual practices into normal and abnormal on the basis of how culturally acceptable they are, we could open up the possibility of delineating them in far more useful ways: in relation to how much pleasure they provide, and how ethical they are, for instance. Denman suggests that the paraphilias should be revisited to distinguish those which are just socially transgressive from those which are *coercive*. She argues that the latter might also more appropriately be dealt with in the realm of criminal justice than psychology or psychiatry.[55] We'll return to some of these ideas in the next chapter.

Rubin's concept of benign variation refers to the kind of sexual diversity approach that I've been emphasising throughout this book: we should regard all sex and sexuality as equally valid and acceptable so long as it is consensual for all concerned.[56] Rubin points out that

> most people find it difficult to grasp that whatever they like to do sexually will be thoroughly repulsive to someone else, and that whatever repels them sexually will be the most treasured delight of someone, somewhere. . . . Most people mistake their sexual preferences for a universal system that will or should work for everyone.[57]

We'll return to Rubin in the conclusion to the chapter. For now let's think a bit further about what's meant by this idea of sexual *consent* that we've been using here.

CONSENT

Non-consensual sex is a serious problem, with around 2.5% of women and 0.4% of men reporting that they've survived an instance of sexual violence in the last year, and 20% of women and 3% of men experiencing some form of sexual offence over the course of their lives, mostly from people who they know. Rates of sexual violence are particularly high for trans people, including non-binary people.[58] Only around 15% of survivors of serious sexual offences report them, demonstrating the high levels of stigma, shame, and fear of disbelief in this area.[59]

Despite this, consent is rarely covered in any depth in sex education or sex advice. In fact, in my analysis of sex advice books I found that the average proportion of books devoted to this topic was only just over 0%, and when it was covered consent was seen as something that was only relevant to people having kinky sex – not sex of other kinds. Consent was never given as an important reason for communicating about sex, or as a topic that people need to communicate about.

Quite a lot of mainstream advice explicitly suggests that people – particularly women – should have sex when they don't want to have it, in order that they'll remain desirable to their partners and keep their relationships 'healthy'. One book claims that women generally don't get into sex until they've been physically stimulated for a while. Another suggests that men are free to do what they want at the moment of orgasm, and that they should surprise their partners by dominating them without discussing it first. This is the really dark side of the sexual imperative because it interferes with people's ability to tune into when they do and don't want sex, and means that they could well be having sex that isn't consensual.[60]

Saying no and saying yes

A common understanding of consent is that sex is consensual if a person doesn't refuse someone's advances or actually say 'no'. However, psychological research in this area has demonstrated that people rarely use the word 'no' in everyday or sexual interactions (being invited to the pub, or being asked for sex). Instead most people follow the cultural convention of trying to let someone down gently, saying things like 'I'm afraid I'm busy tonight', 'I'm not sure', or 'maybe another time'. People generally understand very clearly that these kinds of responses mean that the other person is refusing the invitation, without them actually using the word 'no'.[61]

The 'saying no' approach to consent has been criticized for assuming that consent is present until somebody takes it away. Also the emphasis is on the person receiving the sexual advances, rather than the one making them, reinforcing the cultural tendency to blame sexual assault on the behaviour of the victims (what they are wearing, whether they have been drinking, etc.), rather than the perpetrators.

The 'yes means yes' or 'enthusiastic consent' model is an alternative: each partner is responsible for ensuring that the other is actively enjoying the sexual activity between them, not just 'not saying no' to it, and that it is 'informed consent' so they know what they're getting into.[62] This can also be helpful when differences between people, particularly in terms of culture, class, and neurodiversity, mean that one person might struggle to read another's reluctance. The model can be criticised for suggesting that all consensual sex must be pleasurable to everybody concerned. For example, some asexual people and some sex workers consent to sex without particularly wanting or enjoying it themselves.

Communicative consent

We can also question whether sexual consent can be established in a one-off conversation prior to sex, given that our feelings may change over the course of an interaction. Therefore it needs to be a more active and ongoing process of communicating willingness for sex. This also gets us away from the assumed dynamic of one person actively initiating sex and another person passively accepting it or having to refuse it.

Some people have criticized the communicative consent model as being an unrealistic understanding of how sex generally progresses: they ridicule the idea that you might have to ask for permission for each touch. However, it can certainly include the more common non-verbal forms of sexual communication as well as verbal ones. Melanie Beres gives the example of undoing another person's shirt button. If they proceed to unbutton the rest of their shirt that's clear consent. If they do the button back up or clutch the gap closed, it's not.[63]

However, given the research findings on the lack of communication about sex that we touched on in Chapter 3, we have a long way to go to get to a more communicative consent model.

Consent cultures

Due to the stigmatisation of kink or BDSM as abusive and dangerous, which we touched on earlier, for many years kink communities were at pains to insist that their practices were always 'safe, sane, and consensual'. Unfortunately this had the side effect of driving the non-consensual and abusive dynamics that are present in any community underground. The consent culture movement emerged when people on the BDSM blogosphere started to discuss this more openly, and to think about what might be done to prevent non-consensual and abusive sex.[64]

Many consent culture authors point out how force, control, pressure, persuasion, and manipulation are commonplace in our everyday relationships, such as in our attempts to persuade somebody to attend a social event, or in street harassment when men attempt to engage women in unwanted conversations. These authors ask whether consent is possible in sex if people are engaging in non-consensual practices within the rest of their relationships. For example, in *Fifty Shades of Grey*, Christian never hears Ana's clear 'no' about him buying her gifts, following her on holiday, and getting involved in her work. Also (as in many romantic books and films) both characters continually attempt to pressure, persuade, or cajole the other into being what they want them to be. As blogger The Pervocracy puts it, 'I think part of the reason we have trouble drawing the line "it's not okay to force someone into sexual activity" is that in many ways, forcing people to do things is part of our culture in general. Cut that shit out of your life. If someone doesn't want to go to a party, try a new food, get up and dance, make small talk at the lunchtable – that's their right. Stop the "aww c'mon" and "just this once" and the games where you playfully force someone to play along. Accept that no means no – all the time'.[65]

This links to feminist psychology research which has called attention to the normative heterosexual script we covered in Chapter 3. Nicola Gavey has pointed out how difficult consent can be under power relations where men are assumed to have a natural sex drive and to need sex, while women are not seen as actively desiring beings.[66]

Authors in the consent culture movement agree that there needs to be awareness of both the circulating cultural pressures around sex and the power relations between any two (or more) individuals.[67]

Such awareness needs to be *intersectional*, considering the impact, for example, of age, gender, sexuality, race, nationality, social position, social class, and other differences, on how possible it is for each person to say either 'no' or 'yes' to sex. As activist Pepper Mint points out, non-consensual power dynamics are so common in our schools, workplaces, and wider cultures that 'we are in fact swimming in a soup of non-consensual power dynamics, where our personal strategies are typically shaped by sets of options that can range from mildly undesirable to downright horrific'.[68]

As with recent work on open non-monogamous communities, this kind of work has encouraged kinksters to address the dynamics of privilege and oppression that exist within their communities and the impact this can have,[69] in some cases actively using their sexual practice to increase awareness of these matters.[70]

Based on these ideas we might try to shift to a vision of consent across our culture which:

- Is about finding the overlap between what people actively want, rather than just not doing what they don't want,
- Is an ongoing form of verbal and non-verbal communication,
- Applies to the whole relationship, and to all kinds of relationships, not just to sex and sexual relationships,
- Recognises and addresses the power dynamics which are always in play between people and which make it more difficult for them to freely consent.

CONCLUSION

I hope this chapter has encouraged you to think critically about all models of sex which try to divide people into normal and abnormal (or natural and unnatural, acceptable and unacceptable) on the basis of their sexual desires, identities, relationships, and practices. If we embraced a model of sexual diversity or benign variation, potentially we could put more energy into exploring what works for each individual sexually. We could work on how to ensure that the sex people do have is consensual and ethical, given just how complex this is.

Drawing on what we've covered in this book so far I've imagined a reversal of Rubin's original diagram: one that places benign variation and sexual ethics – including consent – in the centre and that relegates fixed, hierarchical understandings of sex to the outer limits. Before we go on to consider some key current debates in the psychology of sex, think about how you feel about this suggestion as an alternative to the functional/dysfunctional and normal/abnormal divisions.

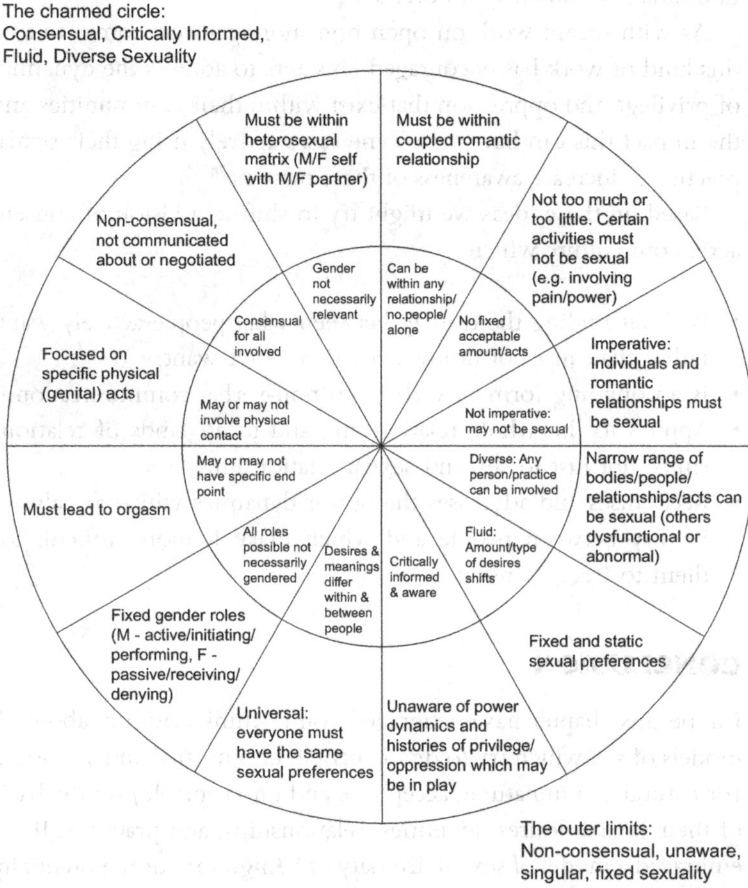

Figure 4.2 Rubin revisited

5

SEXUALISATION!

I hope by this point in the book you've got a pretty good handle on our current cultural understandings around sexuality, what sex is, and hierarchies of sexual and asexual practices and relationships. You should also have a sense of some of the ways in which psychology has been involved in both constructing and challenging prevailing views of sex and sexuality. I hope what we've explored has shown you that psychological knowledge can never completely escape the cultural and personal assumptions of the psychologists involved in producing and presenting it. That includes the knowledge that I've presented in this book, of course.

In this final chapter I want to explore some of the key current debates in sex and sexuality that we haven't already covered. Broadly speaking these fall under the umbrella of 'sexualisation'. This refers to the recent panic that our culture has become 'sexualised' and that this has had a detrimental impact on people.

Sexualisation has been a concern of successive governments, with several attempts to review the evidence on the potentially damaging impact it has, particularly on young people and/or women.[1] In this chapter I'll unpack some of the issues involved in sexualisation before focusing particularly on concerns around the impact on porn, and on sex addiction: both of which have become major topics of psychological focus. After that we'll think a little more about sexual fantasy – a key element underlying these areas which rarely gets considered in the depth it deserves. Finally, we'll return to where we started the book and consider how our sexual identities (or selves) develop within this wider culture that we currently occupy.

The other thing that I want to do in this chapter is to introduce you to a way of thinking critically about such debates that I've found to be helpful. Generally speaking, when people discuss issues such as sexualisation, pornography, or sex addiction in the mainstream media, or even at academic conferences, they polarize into 'for' or 'against'. The underlying question driving the debate is whether this thing we're talking about is a good thing or bad thing: whether it helps people or harms people, or sometimes, as in the case of sex addiction, whether or not it even exists. It's hard not to slip into these binary ways of thinking and talking about issues because they're so entrenched in our culture.

This is a dangerous way of addressing things, however, because it leads to a lot of muddled thinking as well as to the division of people into 'us' and 'them' on the basis of their positions. And of course *we* are the enlightened, rational people with all the objective knowledge on the subject, and *they* are the irrational, biased folks basing their opinions on pseudoscience and opinion. This kind of polarisation is a key element in much human conflict,[2] and it prevents us from listening openly to others and potentially finding our way to more complex and nuanced understandings and smart ways of engaging with the issues that face us.[3]

In this chapter I'll keep asking the following questions. I hope you'll find them useful to apply to other issues and debates as well.

1. What are we talking about here? How is it defined? Is it one thing or many? If it is many things then we need to separate them out and address each element separately.
2. What possibilities does this thing we're talking about open up, and what does it close down? This is a more useful question than 'Is it good or bad?' because it recognises that most things have

the potential to be both. It also keeps our focus on the *impact* of whatever we're concerned about.

3. Given the first two answers, how might we creatively engage with this thing: finding an alternative to either completely embracing it (if we find it good) or attempting to eradicate it (if we find it bad)?

Thinking back over the topics we covered through the rest of the book, I hope you'll see similar themes in the ways that I've tackled, for example, sex advice, sexual practices like BDSM, consent, and so on. When we cover sex addiction in this chapter we'll also return to the issue of diagnosing people with sexual problems with this approach. I find it a very helpful process to guide my thinking when journalists ask me either/or questions such as 'Is *Fifty Shades of Grey* feminist or antifeminist?',[4] 'Is the internet bad or good for relationships?'[5] or 'Is monogamy natural or unnatural?'.[6]

THE SEXUALISATION OF CULTURE[7]

Starting with the topic of sexualisation as a whole, the sexualisation debate has played out in the media, in government policy, and in a number of popular books.[8]

One side of the debate argues that society has become hypersexualised: wherever we go we're blasted with sexual messages. Boys watch hardcore online porn from an early age, which warps their brains and turns them into sexual predators. Girls are sexualised before they're out of toddlerhood with high-heeled baby shoes, Playboy T-shirts, and Barbie or Bratz dolls. By the time they're teenagers they've bought the message from magazines and music videos that being sexy is all-important, putting them at risk of everything from eating disorders to STIs and teen pregnancy to sexual violence.

The other side of the debate emphasises choice and fun and power. It argues that we live in a time of gender equality where everyone gets to choose who they want to be, and if women want to go pole-dancing for leisure and feel empowered by dressing up sexy that's great. It claims that sexualisation is a moral panic: the kind of thing people get worked up about every decade or so. Weren't people panicking about miniskirts and rock & roll in the same ways back in the 1950s and 1960s?

You might like to reflect on whether you're familiar with these debates in any form. What position have you taken in them to date? You might find it useful to go back to the three questions in the introduction to this chapter and consider them before reading on.

What do we mean by sexualisation?

I hope you can see from the overview of the debate that part of the problem is that people use the umbrella term 'sexualisation' to refer to a multitude of different things. They are concerned with many different kinds of media and practices (music videos, lads' mags, toys, clothes, porn, sexting) and with many different possible effects (gender violence, STI transmission, sexual bullying, gender roles, child sexual abuse).

When Robbie Duchinsky and I analysed the government reports in this area we found that they used the term 'sexualisation' to refer to both media content and practices that do the following four things.[9]

1. Being sexually suggestive
2. Being sexist and treating women as sexual only or as sex objects
3. Encouraging children to think of themselves as adult or sexual – or inducing other people to think of children in this way
4. Glamorising or normalising deviant behaviour

When these four faces of sexualisation are conflated it makes debate difficult because disagreeing with any one of them seems like you're disagreeing with all of them. For example, a person might be concerned about girls being encouraged from an early age to be sexually desirable to boys as a key part of their identity, and with very restricted ideals about what kind of appearance is desirable. However, that same person might also have real problems with attempts to censor depictions of 'deviant behaviour' given what we know about the impact of sex hierarchies (see Chapter 4) and concerns around freedom of speech. When sexualisation is presented by either side as just one thing to be for or against, it makes such positions difficult to hold and to articulate. Concern about all four aspects of sexualisation together, or dismissal of them, is presented as 'common sense'.

So it would be useful, whenever we're talking about sexualisation, to define specifically *which* aspect we're speaking about, and what potential effect we're trying to determine. For example, a more helpful question than 'Is sexualisation harming our society?' would be: 'Are children watching sexual online materials and if they are, what effect does that have on them?' or 'Do men's magazines present women in objectifying ways, and if they do, does this influence reader attitudes and behaviour around gender and sex?'

What does it open up and close down?

Once we get specific we can also look at each example from the point of view of what it opens up and what it closes down. Instead of assuming that kids watching sexual content, or men reading lads' mags is *either* good *or* bad, we can consider the potential that they may be positive in some ways and negative in others. We can recognise the inevitable tensions and contradictions that exist in the complex world we live in.

First of all, we know that media affects different people in different ways – otherwise we'd all love and hate the same films, TV programmes, and music.[10] So we can't generalise about any particular media 'effect'. Rather, we need to explore how different audiences relate to such content, recognising that some may accept what it says uncritically, others may be relatively neutral towards it, and others may resist its messages. For example, Clare Bale has researched how kids relate to sexual online content in various ways, including ridicule and critical analysis;[11] David Gauntlett has examined how lads' mags can both perpetuate problematic forms of masculinity *and* open up possibilities for men to access more emotional expression or support.[12]

We're massively shaped by the world around us, so the current level of sexual imagery is unlikely to leave any of us untouched. We also all filter this through our own experiences and histories in unique ways, so that the same messages won't have the same impact on everybody. For this reason it's also useful for us to reflect on our own experiences and agendas in these kinds of debates. What do we bring to them? We could acknowledge that being someone who watches porn, and/or a parent, and/or a person who does or does not fit the current ideals of sexiness, all influence how we come to the debates. We could also recognise that whoever we're arguing with will likely have similar deeply personal investments in it.

Creative engagement

Once we have a better understanding of what each aspect of sexualisation opens up and closes down then we're in a better position to creatively engage with it. We might find that a certain form of media does have a detrimental impact on young people, but also that many of them really love that media. That would lead to us thinking carefully about what it is they're getting out of it, how we might make media with different messages equally appealing, or enable a more critical engagement from the young people themselves.

Such mindful reflection should also help us to ask important questions about what the current concerns and debates reveal and obscure, what is included and what is excluded. For example, in our paper Robbie and I noticed that the parents who were interviewed for the report on the sexualisation of childhood were equally concerned about the impact of *sexualised* toys and clothes on their kids, and the impact of *gender-stereotyped* toys and clothes. However, the report claimed that the former was a grave concern with a major impact, while the latter was dismissed as inevitable, with gender preferences presented as a natural part of 'normal, healthy development of gender identity'. Again, this is an example of policy documents – and the psychological work they draw upon – constructing a certain reality. Many readings of the evidence would suggest that gender stereotyping has at least as detrimental effect on children of all genders as sexualisation does.[13]

The sexualisation reports and debate often make a cultural assumption of childhood innocence which can be tainted by media and products. This is a problem because it can mean that childhood sexuality is denied or regarded as inevitably problematic. Also children who don't follow an 'appropriate' – often heterosexual white middle-class – trajectory from childhood to adulthood are stigmatised or demonised.[14] Ironically, cultural concerns over sex and childhood can mean *poorer* sex education because we become so anxious about talking to kids about sex. This often means that young people are actually *more* driven to seek out sexual media in order to inform themselves about sex.[15] With a lack of decent information, young people may be more at risk of failing to understand when they are being sexually abused or coerced. Also the huge focus on the sexual behaviour of children may mean that we pay less attention to the other forms of bullying, violence, and abuse which are a major part of many young people's lives and have a devastating impact.[16]

We've only scratched the surface of the different meanings of sexualisation here, and what psychological research and theory has to say about them. Check out The Sexualization Report online for more information on all the four faces of sexualisation written by people with various positions on the debate.[17]

PORN PANIC

One specific concern within the sexualisation debates has been the impact of pornography. Before we go on, you might like to think about your own position on porn. Is it something you've engaged with? What views do you have on porn in general, and on different forms of sexual media? Again you might like to reflect on the three questions in the introduction to this chapter in relation to porn.

Mainstream psychology has engaged with the impact of pornography many times over the years;[18] however, it often runs into methodological problems. There's no one perfect kind of research we could do to tell us the effects of reading or watching porn. Some psychologists have shown students porn in a lab and studied whether they give somebody more electric shocks, or score differently on measures of sexist attitudes, afterwards. But there are issues about whether the findings of such studies would apply to other kinds of people in real world contexts. Others have investigated whether countries with more porn have higher levels of sexual violence, for example. But even if they did we can't be sure whether the porn caused the violence, or violent people bought more porn, or whether some other aspect (such as wider cultural norms around masculinity)[19] was responsible for both the higher interest in porn and the sexual violence. It's the classic correlation-doesn't-equal-causation problem.[20] Other psychologists have asked sex offenders about their usage of porn, but offenders might not give honest answers, and – again – we can't be sure whether those who looked at porn did so *because* of their tastes in sexual violence, or whether it *caused* that.

When psychologists review the results of all of these different kinds of research, the results are inconsistent. Some lab experiments do show effects of *violent* pornography on men's attitudes towards women and on aggression, but other forms of porn have no effects, or even opposite ones.[21] Countries where porn has become more easily accessible generally show no increase in sex crimes.[22] Sex offenders often had less, and later, exposure to porn than other kinds of offenders.[23]

What do we mean by porn?

As with sexualisation, it's important to start by defining what we mean by porn.[24] Some of the inconsistencies in the research findings might be explained because psychologists have included different things as porn, in addition to studying their impact on different groups of people and in different contexts.

The legal definition of pornography in Britain is materials 'produced solely or principally for the purposes of sexual arousal'.[25] Obviously that includes a vast array of different things, from photo shoots in magazines, to *Fifty Shades of Grey*, to mainstream porn clips, to violent sexual images, to sexting,[26] to feminist porn vids,[27] and a great deal more. It's often said that the line between erotica and porn is very much dependent on the tastes of whoever is doing the defining.[28] Even if we focus in on violent or extreme pornography[29] it's very difficult to pin down. Current definitions could include images of consensual BDSM practices akin to acupuncture, for example (see Chapter 4), but not 'torture porn' movies like *Saw* or *Hostel* because those are mainstream films which don't explicitly aim to sexually arouse.

As lawyer Myles Jackman[30] points out, context can mean that something which wasn't intended as porn becomes so (e.g. if the torture scene from *Casino Royale* was edited together with similar scenes from other movies), or that something that was pornographic ceases to be so (e.g. viral porn movie clips which are circulated for shock or humour value rather than to produce sexual arousal).[31]

What does it open up and close down?

Just as there are many different kinds of porn, people often engage with porn for many different reasons.[32] The meanings that porn has for people, and the ways they engage with it, may well be very important in determining whether they find it to be a positive, negative, or neutral thing in their lives, or all of these things.

As with sexualisation, more focused and nuanced research is needed. Research suggests, for example, that those who engage with online porn have both more relationship problems *and* better sexual knowledge and attitudes.[33] Aleksandra Antevska and Nicola Gavey's in-depth interviews with young men who viewed mainstream porn found that most of them downplayed the sexism involved in the standard dominant men/submissive women script with its focus on male sexual pleasure and extreme sexual acts. However, a minority of the men critically reflected on the ethical dilemmas posed by what they were viewing.[34] Rachael Liberman's conversations with producers and consumers of feminist porn found that they saw it as a more explicitly ethical alternative to mainstream porn, which helped them to actively explore different sexual practices and identities.[35]

Alan McKee and his colleagues found that porn helps young people to develop several key aspects of healthy sexual development[36] such as learning what they might enjoy, self-acceptance, open communication with partners, and feeling that sex can be pleasurable and joyful rather than aggressive and coercive (depictions of joyless sex are not popular with most porn viewers). Porn is, however, also bad at promoting the healthy sexual development features of consensual negotiation of sex, safer sex, public/private boundaries, and relationship skills.[37]

Creative engagement

This more complex and nuanced kind of research gives us some pointers about how we might creatively engage with the existence of pornography. For example, what might we learn from the young men who *do* engage critically with mainstream porn about what encourages them to do so, and from producers and consumers of feminist and ethical porn about what is possible in sex media?

The research of McKee and his colleagues highlights the fact that good sex and relationship education and advice are essential for plugging the gaps in the areas where porn is poor at promoting healthy sexual development. Unfortunately, though, despite evidence for its effectiveness,[38] SRE rarely seems to be high on government agenda, and frequently focuses on safer PIV sex, rather than on gender and sexual diversity and issues such as consent, communication, relationships, and pleasure, which is what young people are most concerned with.[39]

As with sexualisation, we can ask useful questions about the focus on porn as an explanation for various problems by mainstream media and politicians, in the criminal justice system, and by psychology. What does this focus on porn obscure or exclude?

As with many examples of blaming specific media,[40] porn *can* be a handy cultural scapegoat. It enables us to focus on an evil outside force, rather than asking more uncomfortable questions about the role of structural inequalities (in which we are all implicated) in crime.[41] It also focuses attention away from the problematic ideas about sex, gender, and violence that are around us all of the time[42] in mainstream media and in everyday conversations.[43] For example, instead of concentrating on porn we might worry just as much about the impact of the messages in sex advice about the kind of sex people *should* be having (see Chapters 3 & 4), in women's magazines about how women should look and behave,[44] and in men's magazines where rape myths are frequently perpetuated.[45] We could also usefully examine the problematic ideas that are present in court cases[46] and political debates[47] themselves. To tackle the problems of sexism, narrow representations of sex, and sexual violence and abuse, we need to cast the net a lot wider than porn alone.

SEX ADDICTS

Another recent concern falling under the wider umbrella of sexualisation is sex addiction: the idea that many people (especially men) are becoming addicted to sex. This is said to be causing relationship problems and breakdown, financial difficulties and job losses, and rises in STI infection and unplanned pregnancies.[48] There are particular anxieties that addiction to internet porn and online sex are on the increase, and that these are addictive in a way similar to drugs and alcohol, altering brain structure and chemistry such that people can no longer gain pleasure from other forms of sex.

While lack of agreement in this area means that sex addiction, or 'hypersexual disorder', has not been added to the DSM list of sexual dysfunctions (see Chapter 3),[49] many psychologists and psychotherapists have set themselves up as experts in sex addiction,[50] offering services to treat sex addicts. Sex addiction is listed as a common sexual problem by recognised sex and relationship therapy organisations.

What do we mean by sex addiction?

This proposed diagnostic term, 'hypersexual disorder', gives us a clue to the meaning of sex addiction. If 'hypoactive sexual desire disorder' refers to desire being too low (see Chapter 3), then 'hypersexual' refers to it being too high. Paul Joannides argues that psychiatrists and psychotherapists are basing their ideas on a 'Goldilocks' amount of sex (not too little and not too much). But the 'appropriate level' varies greatly between individual practitioners and theoretical approaches. He gives the example of one study which regarded masturbation due to loneliness as a sign of sexual addiction. He asks, what level of loneliness is acceptable in life? And who determines the 'correct' reasons for masturbation?[51] Some people have suggested that the Goldilocks amount of sex is generally the amount of sex that the practitioner is having themselves!

Some more insight into what therapists mean by sex addiction can be found if we look at the definitions given by major sex therapy bodies. One includes the following list:

> While many people with no sexual behavioural problem may take part in the activities below, signs of sexual addiction may include:
>
> - Compulsive masturbation (self-stimulation)
> - Multiple affairs (extra-marital affairs)
> - Multiple or anonymous sexual partners and/or one-night stands
> - Consistent use of pornography
> - Unsafe sex
> - Phone or computer sex (cybersex)
> - Prostitution or use of prostitutes
> - Exhibitionism
> - Obsessive dating through personal ads
> - Sexual harassment
> - Voyeurism (watching others) and/or stalking
> - Law breaking[52]

Having read Chapter 4 I hope you'll immediately see some issues with this list, along the lines of the ones we discussed concerning the criteria for paraphilic disorders. Here we are first given the proviso that these things are only a problem if they are *experienced* as problematic. However, as we know, there's the dangerous feedback loop that the very fact of listing behaviours as signs of sex addiction or disorder stigmatises them further, meaning that people are more likely to feel ashamed and bad about them. There's also the usual slippage between transgressive and coercive practices here, and a sense that 'outer limits' sexual practices are far more likely to be addictive than those in the 'charmed circle'. The link with addiction further stigmatises groups and practices which are already marginalised enough in our culture. Little thought is given to the potential impact of this on those who engage in solo sex, online sex, non-monogamy, or sex work.[53] Critics have also pointed out that some of these practices are particularly common among gay men, so there's a real risk that this becomes a new way of pathologising them, now that homosexuality itself is no longer classed as a disorder.[54]

Finally it's clear that, like sexualisation and porn, sex addiction is an umbrella term that covers many different things. Does it make sense to lump together people who continually seek out the hot intensity of new relationship energy (sex and love addiction), with people who spend long periods masturbating to porn mags, with those who have many casual sexual partners, with those who find webcam sex online compulsive, with those who are having an affair, and so on?

What does it open up and close down?

There are many reasons to be cautious about diagnosing somebody as a sex addict. In addition to the issues of coherence, we might question whether there is *really* any increase in sex addiction, or whether it is more an increase in the popularity of the term and people being encouraged to be concerned about these behaviours.[55] Remembering back to Chapter 2 we might point out that *everything* we do influences our brains – so the insistence that an effect is 'real' because it causes brain changes is questionable, to say the least.[56]

It is certainly the case that some people *do* experience problems with their sexual desires and practices, feeling compelled to spend a lot of time and energy on forms of sex which interfere with other aspects of their lives, or which they feel uncomfortable or distressed about, or which put them at risk in various ways.

If somebody regards themself as a sex addict, it's important to clarify what this person *means* by sex addiction. The second of our questions is also useful: What does the label of sex addict open up and close down for them? It could be just as disempowering to dismiss a person's sense of themself as a sex addict as it would be to accept it without question. If, instead, we explore the pros and cons of such a label people can hold it more openly: recognising the struggles they are having, but not grasping the idea that they must be 'sex addicts' as some kind of fixed identity.

When I've had this kind of conversation with clients they've said that the label 'sex addict' gives them the sense that there's something real going on for them, that they're not simply to blame for it, and that there are other people struggling in the same way who they could get support and understanding from. However, they often worry that the label of 'sex addict' will stick to them; that being a sex addict means that there's no possibility for change; that it doesn't recognise the uniqueness of their experience which is not identical to everyone else's; and that if they're diagnosed in this way people won't acknowledge what it is that is so compelling and important for them about the sex they are pursuing – even if it does cause problems.[57]

Creative engagement

When creatively engaging with a person who's struggling with 'sex addiction' it's important to discuss the cultural messages they've received about sex. Is this thing a problem because it's upsetting them, or is it a problem because society sees it as 'bad' or because other people in their life have a problem with it? Obviously these things aren't always easy to disentangle.[58]

It's also useful to keep 'opening up and closing down' in mind. While what they're doing is obviously distressing (given they're seeking help for it), it also must be giving them something too in order to be so compelling to them. We might usefully explore both the losses and the gains involved. As with the other kinds of sexual problems we covered in Chapter 2, a key thing here is to explore the multiple *meanings* that the 'sex addiction' has for the individual person. For example, I've worked with two young men who spent a lot of their time on online sexual encounters. However, what they got out of it couldn't have been more different. For one it was a soothing activity where he could escape from the tough realities of his life into a kind of black hole where he didn't have to feel anxious. For the other, it was the place he felt most alive and awake: cybersex enabled him to unleash a confident, dominant persona that he couldn't let himself be in the rest of his life, and to express the kind of creativity that wasn't possible in his dull job.

Some conventional 'treatments' for addiction involve abstinence: people simply stopping the problematic behaviour. This risks not allowing people to become aware of what their behaviour *means* to them, and what they *gain* from it. Also people often end up swinging from complete abstinence to going back to the compulsion – and feeling terrible about it. The mindfulness idea of 'being present' is useful here. Instead of losing ourselves in the behaviour, or trying to avoid it completely, we can engage in it in a slower, more self-aware way, reflecting afterwards about what was so compelling about it for us.[59]

We'll look at the meanings of sexual desires in more detail in the next section because it can be useful to explore them in this kind of way whether or not we experience them as problematic.

THE EROTIC IMAGINATION

As we've seen, there's a tendency in psychology to draw dividing lines between porn and erotica. We also tend to distinguish between people consuming sexual materials that other people have created, and those who use their own erotic thoughts and imaginings. There's a value to exploring this whole realm of sexual fantasy together: considering what our sexual desires are, (however we go about engaging with them) and the meanings that they might have for us.

Common sexual fantasies

As we saw in the last chapter, many of the sexual desires that have been labelled 'abnormal' are actually very common. Christian Joyal and his colleagues have recently studied the popularity of diverse sexual fantasies.[60] They found, for example, that over 80% of people fantasized about sex in unusual places, and over 70% about sex with somebody other than their partner. Over 50% fantasized about group sex of some kind, and a similar proportion included some form of BDSM in their fantasies. Forms of exhibitionism, voyeurism, masturbation, oral and anal sex were also popular fantasies, as was sex with a celebrity. Popular collections of people's sexual fantasies generally include many of these as major themes as well. They are a useful read for people who are looking to explore their own sexual desires, and they can helpfully normalise the experiences of people who have been worrying about the nature of their desires.[61]

The meaning of fantasies

A few psychotherapists have endeavoured to conduct more in-depth analyses of fantasies to explore both common content and what we can learn about ourselves by tuning into our fantasies.[62] These authors don't propose any *universal* meanings of fantasies. Rather, like dreams, fantasies have unique meanings which we can tap into if we reflect on various elements of the fantasies and how they operate for us.

In the 1990s US humanistic therapist Jack Morin wrote *The Erotic Mind*, based on his 'sexual excitement survey' with hundreds of people, as well as detailed analysis of the specific sexual fantasies of many of his clients.[63] In the 2000s UK psychoanalyst Brett Kahr conducted an even more extensive survey of nearly 20,000 people in total, including thousands of survey responses and over a hundred in-depth interviews about people's lives and fantasies. This research formed the basis of his book *Sex and The Psyche*.[64]

It's interesting to compare how therapists from these different approaches – humanistic and psychoanalytic – make sense of sexual fantasies. They definitely agree that our recurring fantasies are often rooted in our key childhood and adolescent experiences, and have much to tell us about our hopes, fears, conflicts, and values. Kahr, however, often slips into quite pathologising language (see Chapter 4) and focuses on traumatic past experiences, whereas Morin takes a perspective which has more in common with the idea of sexual diversity or benign variation (see Chapter 4) and takes peak pleasurable erotic experiences as his starting point. Both of these books are well worth a read, and include material that can help you to explore and expand your own erotic imagination. Here I'll just touch on a few of the key ideas that they discuss.

Kahr and Morin agree that virtually everyone *does* fantasize, whether it's as simple as picturing a specific person or sex act when you get turned on, or as complex as creating an ongoing detailed sexual story in your mind. Before we go on, think about whether you have recurring sexual fantasies. What are your favourite ones? You might find it useful to write them down so that you can think about them in relation to Kahr's and Morin's ideas.

Morin proposes an erotic equation: Excitement = Attraction + Obstacles. In other words, we tend to find it arousing when we're attracted to something *and* there's some difficulty to be overcome in order to get it. For example, a common theme in erotic fan fiction is the 'first time' story, where it isn't clear whether a character's attraction is reciprocated, but it turns out that it is when they've been brave enough to confess. Also common are 'hurt comfort' stories, where a person has to endure some pain to get to the pleasure. There are also common themes of people having taboo desires (same-sex attraction or BDSM, for example) which are then fulfilled.[65] In a simpler form, Morin's equation perhaps explains why partially clothed can be sexier than completely naked! It also relates back to Esther Perel's work about maintaining passion in long-term relationships (see Chapter 3): she suggests that it's hard to get warmth and heat in the same place. Perhaps warm close relationships don't provide us with enough sense of an obstacle to be exciting.[66] Paradoxically Morin finds the things that can get in the way of desire – like anxiety, guilt, and anger – can also amplify it, in small doses.

Past and present patterns

For Morin and Kahn this all gives a clue to where our core erotic themes come from. While we're rarely conscious of it, we seem to use sexual fantasies to transform the obstacles of emotionally tough experiences from our past into excitement and pleasure. Both authors give many powerful examples where a person describes a compelling fantasy which makes no sense to them, but probing into their past makes it crystal clear. For example, a person who experienced lots of unrequited love might fantasize about being in the midst of an orgy, utterly desired by all, or whisked away by a romantic hero. Someone who was bullied and rejected at school might turn the tables and be the dominant one in their fantasies, or they might imagine similar scenarios to the bullying but where it is consensual and pleasurable for them to submit. A person who was shamed for their bodily functions in the past may imagine pissing on other people, or being carefully washed clean after such a thing happened to them. As you can see, different experiences seem to lodge in the erotic minds of different people, and fantasies operate in uniquely personal ways in order to address them.

So tuning into your sexual fantasies can be a good way of tuning into what you enjoy sexually; it can also provide insights into some of your key patterns in life, which can be helpful to explore and perhaps shift. Consider the two examples I gave earlier of self-diagnosed 'sex addicts'. The one who loved playing the dominant in his fantasies and in cybersex realised that earlier experiences of being shamed when he was creative had made him restrict his creativity to the erotic arena. Gradually he found it useful to experiment with bringing more creativity into his work and relationships. It was useful for him to understand why it was so scary for him to do so. The other man who was struggling with online sex was initially very reluctant to look at the actual content of what excited him. We explored how, by metaphorically walling them off in a separate part of his mind that he refused to look at, his fantasies only became louder and more fearsome. When he was able to open up to himself about the appeal of porn depicting the domination of women or younger people, he was surprised to realise that he himself identified with the submissive people in the scenarios, not the dominant ones. This linked back, for him, to feeling that his own developing sexuality had been wrestled away from him by older kids at school pressuring him into watching porn and being sexual. Not only did this enable him to consider more ethical ways of exploring his sexuality online, it also lead to useful explorations of the way being controlled by others played out in other aspects of his life.

As Morin warns, the main danger with turn-ons which disturb us arises when we try to deny them and hide them from ourselves. When we do that they can spill over in uncontrollable ways. Turning towards them with openness and curiosity can enable self-understanding and aware decisions about how we might engage with, and even expand, our fantasies.[67]

Of course it is worth thinking critically about Kahr and Morin's ideas as well. Are all fantasies rooted in our relationship to the painful obstacles of life? Other research finds that quite a lot of people link their fantasy themes to media they enjoyed as kids, such as watching somebody get tied up on *Star Trek* or *Doctor Who*, which seems to be more about pleasant than painful memories.[68] Are all fantasies rooted in the distant past? What about somebody who only starts fantasizing about having relationships with people who are younger than they are once they feel like they are getting old? I suspect Morin or Kahr would suggest that these themes were only appealing because they related to desires to be controlled, or to be found attractive by attractive people, which *were* rooted in past tough experiences. But as psychologists so often say, there's a need for a lot more research in this area before we can be sure!

SEXUAL SELVES

Now that we've considered sex and sexuality from so many different angles I thought it would be useful to end the book by bringing it all together with the question of how we become the sexual selves that we are, with our unique arrays of desires, identities, attitudes, and sexual practices. As we began our explorations in Chapter 2, the answer has got to be a complex, dynamic, ongoing biopsychosocial process with our wider culture, personal experiences, and brain and body configuration continually influencing each other to shape who we become.

Several sociologists have shed light on how cultural aspects operate in this process. These are useful theories if we want to understand the current impact of 'sexualisation'. John Gagnon and William Simon proposed that we each develop our own *sexual scripts* through the interaction between our wider society, our interpersonal experiences, and our intrapsychic lives.[69]

Sexual script theory

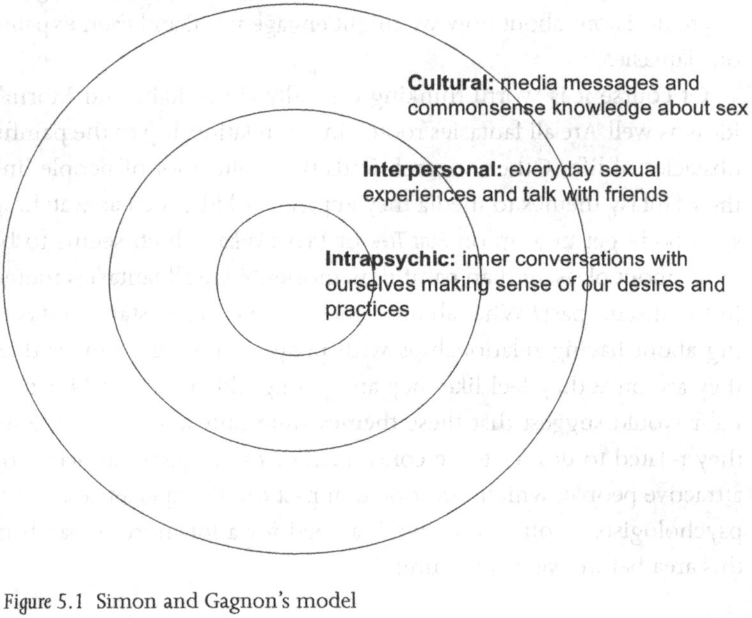

Figure 5.1 Simon and Gagnon's model

Humanistic psychotherapists like Jack Morin might add an extra 'existential' layer beyond the cultural one, for the universal themes which all humans grapple with, which consistently seem to reveal themselves through our sexual desires: themes such as security vs. freedom, being controlled vs. controlling others, fear of death, and the search for meaning.[70]

Our *culture* then determines the meanings that are available to us – in our time and place – around sex. Our *interpersonal* experiences situate us within those meanings, and also shape how we relate to the existential themes. And at the *intrapsychic* level, certain desires emerge in relation to these experiences and cultural messages, and we also have more conscious thoughts: for example, about which desires to act upon and be open about and which not.

Sexual stories

Sociologist Ken Plummer[71] developed Simon and Gagnon's ideas of how culture is involved in our sexual self in his theory of *sexual stories*. He says that we all tell stories about ourselves: narratives about who we are and how we came to be that way, which we repeat to ourselves (intrapsychic) and others (interpersonal) to make sense of our lives and to present ourselves in certain – often favourable – ways. Frequently these narratives draw on the stories that are available to us in the media and the communities we inhabit (culture).

Plummer suggests that in recent decades sex has become the 'big story', with people being encouraged to tell tales of their sexual behaviour and identity, such as the 'rape survivor' story or the 'coming out' story. These stories are told on talk shows, in magazines and newspapers, over telephone help lines, and in support groups. This means that such stories often take on similar structures and contain the same key elements. For example, coming out stories often begin with somebody recognising that they were 'different' in some way as a child or teenager and progress through their realisation that there were others like them, and them putting a name to their difference.

Sexual stories aren't told in isolation, but interpersonally and socially, with different individuals, groups, or organisations being involved in the stories in various ways. These include: the *storytellers* themselves (e.g. participants in research projects or on talk shows), the *coaxers, coachers and coercers* who have the power to elicit stories from the tellers (e.g. the therapist or journalist), and the *consumers* of the story (e.g. TV audiences or readers of newspaper reports about research). Of course some consumers will also be storytellers themselves, and the stories that they read and hear will influence the stories which they, themselves, tell. Social media has perhaps blurred the boundaries between storytellers, coaxers, and consumers even more.

Plummer argues that through this kind of process different sexual stories come to have their *time* in the spotlight: when there is a critical mass of people willing to tell their stories, people wanting to elicit them, and a thirst to consume them. You can see this in the discussions we've had about BDSM, polyamory, sex addiction, asexuality, and trans- and non-binary gender elsewhere in the book. Each have had moments of peak interest in the last decade or so. It's also clear that the kinds of stories that have been widely told about each of these things shape the ways in which other people identifying themselves in these ways tell their own stories. Studying these areas over time you can also see several *waves* of interest, each of which open up new possible stories (as with the shifting stories about BDSM and open non-monogamy that we covered in Chapter 4).

Sexual subjects

Bringing this back to the current sexual moment – the supposed sexualisation of culture: while we can be critical of everything that is lumped together under this umbrella, there's certainly a sense that we're encouraged or coaxed to be particular kinds of sexual selves these days.

For a start, as we saw in Chapter 2, over the last century we've been increasingly encouraged to regard ourselves as having a fixed sexual identity which we need to be 'out' about with others in our world in order to be healthy human beings. There's also been the trend towards having sex for pleasure and leisure, which left us with the sexual imperative that we discussed in Chapter 3. Then, in the last couple of decades, there's been a shift towards what feminist psychologist Rosalind Gill[72] calls sexual subjectification.[73]

Subjectification refers to a wider societal shift from others policing us toward us policing ourselves in various ways: for example, from homosexuality being punished as a crime or pathologised by psychiatrists (see Chapter 2), to gay men monitoring themselves to check whether they match up to the kind of 'good gay citizen' that they see in the media: one who gets married, is stereotypically masculine, and is not 'too overt' about his sexual practices.[74]

Gill focuses on women's sexuality. She says that the shift to subjectification has been from women being policed by the *male gaze* to them policing themselves through constant self-surveillance and self-perfection. Gill looks at recent shifts, for example, in advertising for underwear, in women's magazines, and in romance fiction aimed at women. She demonstrates that there has been a marked change from the previous 'objectification' of women, where attractive women's bodies were used to sell products and women were presented as passively waiting to be swept off their feet. Current 'subjectification' instead depicts women as autonomously choosing to be sexual in 'empowering' and 'playful' ways.

Women are encouraged to beautify themselves for their own pleasure rather than to please men, and their desirability is depicted as a kind of power over men, as in recent bra adverts where the viewer is the woman entering a room and everybody in the advert is turning to look at them with a desiring gaze.[75] However, the women in these images still look very much like the objects of male desire of earlier decades (thin, young, unblemished, etc.), and the women in 'chick lit' novels are still overwhelmingly depicted as needing a romantic relationship with a man to make them complete.[76]

All this emphasis on choice, fun and power also makes it very difficult for people to resist messages about sexiness. To be a lad means always being up for it, and to be an empowered woman means choosing to pamper yourself so you look gorgeous and have all eyes on you. There's no room for all the many men who feel anxious about sex, or women who don't fit the very rigid standards of youth and beauty. And those that do fit live in fear of losing those things. Of course such fears are an excellent way of selling beauty products, self-help books, makeover TV programmes, this season's fashion, and any number of other products.[77]

As we saw in the previous two chapters, these messages also mean that people are walking a tightrope trying to have sex that is both 'normal' and 'great' without straying beyond the current boundaries of acceptability into sex addiction or sluttiness on one side, or sexual dysfunction or boredom on the other. The sex hierarchy might have altered over the years, but it's still very much in place.

We might usefully consider what creative engagement with this current sexual context would look like. For me it definitely involves increasing awareness among people about all the forces which shape their identities and practices, and encouraging critical engagement with the social worlds they are embedded in, and with their own desires and experiences within this.

CONCLUSIONS

I hope this chapter has given you a good sense of current issues regarding the cultural messages we receive about sex, as well as some tools for thinking critically about debates in these areas. Something else you might find useful for this is the 'bad sex media bingo' card which a group of us put together to encourage people to engage critically with media representations of the kinds of topics covered in this chapter.[78] The website links to a play-along copy of the bingo card and the reasons why each of the squares is a problematic depiction. Try having a go next time you watch a documentary or read an article about sex.

You've also delved deeper in this chapter into questions of where our sexual desires come from and how our sexual selves are shaped through our lives and the world around us. Again, it'd be helpful to reflect on your own desires, and the stories you tell yourselves and others about your sexuality and sexual experiences, to help you evaluate the various theories we've covered. To what extent can you see your early struggles in the content of your sexual fantasies? How have wider sexual stories influenced your own narratives and sexual scripts? Can you see the cultural shift to sexual subjectification playing out in your own life and relationships?

FURTHER RESOURCES

Throughout this book I've tried to provide you with useful suggestions for accessible further reading on each of the topics we've covered. Here I'll pull out a few books and websites that are particularly helpful if you want to find out more about sex and sexuality from various perspectives.

MY BOOKS

I've written a few other books myself which tackle topics and themes from this book in more depth.

If you want to read more about how you might apply these kinds of ideas to your own sex life this book covers it:

Barker, M.-J., & Hancock, J. (2016). *Enjoy sex (How, when and if you want to): A practical and inclusive guide / Sex: A practical guide*. London: Icon Books.

If you're interested in some of the theories I've introduced here from beyond psychology, or more about queer in particular, this is an accessible overview:

Barker, M.-J., & Scheele, J. (2016). *Queer: A graphic history/Introducing queer theory*. London: Icon Books.

If you're interested in relationships more widely than just the sexual side of things, this is my book on that topic.

Barker, M.-J. (2018). *Rewriting the rules: An anti-self-help guide to love, sex and relationships.* London: Routledge.

If you're interested in following up the ideas in here about gender, this is a good bet:

Iantaffi, A., & Barker, M.-J. (2017). *How to understand your gender: A practical guide for exploring who you are.* London: Jessica Kingsley.

MORE ON SEXUALITY

There are a few useful introductions to sex and sexuality from different starting points which you might find helpful:

Two short introductions to the sociology and history of sexuality are:

Mottier, V. (2008). *Sexuality: A very short introduction.* Oxford: Oxford University Press.

and

Weeks, J. (2004). *Sexuality: Key ideas.* London: Routledge.

If you're interested in more on the biopsychosocial approach try:

Denman, C. (2003). *Sexuality: A biopsychosocial approach.* Basingstoke: Palgrave Macmillan.

and

Fausto-Sterling, A. (2012). *Sex/gender: Biology in a social world.* New York: Routledge.

For a more mainstream psychology textbook on human sexuality, Justin Lehmiller's book is comprehensive and up to date:

Lehmiller, J. J. (2013). *The psychology of human sexuality.* London: John Wiley & Sons.

To explore global perspectives of sex and sexuality further, this academic book is useful:

Aggleton, P., Boyce, P., Moore, H. L., & Parker, R. (Ed.). (2012). *Understanding global sexualities: New frontiers*. London: Routledge.

Finally, the following are popular books that explore some similar territory to this book, but from different angles, and focusing on different aspects.

Bering, J. (2014). *Perv: The sexual deviant in all of us*. London: Transworld Digital.

de Botton, A. (2012). *How to think more about sex*. London: Macmillan.

Magnanti, B. (2012). *The sex myth: Why everything we're told is wrong*. London: Weidenfeld & Nicolson.

Roach, M. (2009). *Bonk: The curious coupling of sex and science*. London: Canongate Books.

Spiegelhalter, D. (2015). *Sex by numbers: What statistics can tell us about sexual behaviour*. London: Profile Books.

WEBSITES

I list many other useful websites on my own site at www.rewriting-the-rules.com, but here are a few particularly helpful ones.

Justin Hancock and I blog, podcast, and produce zines about sex and relationships on megjohnandjustin.com.

Justin Lehmiller has a blog covering psychological research on sex and sexuality at www.lehmiller.com

Psychology Today often includes articles on sex-related topics, for example Elizabeth Sheff's column on polyamory:

www.psychologytoday.com/topics/sex
www.psychologytoday.com/blog/the-polyamorists-next-door

There are many good TED talks about sex and sexuality:

www.ted.com/topics/sex

The Sexualization Report, Onscenity, and Bad Sex Media Bingo websites are all good places to find out more about the topics covered in the latter part of this book:

thesexualizationreport.wordpress.com

www.onscenity.org
badsexmediabingo.com

For more academic papers, the Taylor & Francis journal *Psychology & Sexuality*, which Darren Langdridge and I co-founded, has a good collection of articles on these topics: www.tandfonline.com/toc/rpse20/current

The British Psychological Society also has a *Psychology of Sexualities* section which produces a journal, reports, etc.: www.bps.org.uk/psychology-public/areas-psychology/psychology-sexualities-section

NOTES

CHAPTER 1

1 When I'm talking about psychology in this book I'm generally referring to western psychology within a western cultural context. There's a lot of scope in this area for engaging with psychologies that have developed in other cultural contexts, as well as with the vast cultural diversity that exists in understandings of sex and sexuality. However, sadly this is something that hasn't happened much in the psychology of sex to date, so I won't cover it in depth in this book. The further reading at the end will give you some pointers if you're interested in exploring this more.

2 There's a nice overview of some of these studies here: www.simplypsychology.org/primacy-recency.html

3 You can read about this study, and some reflections on it here: www.theatlantic.com/health/archive/2015/01/rethinking-one-of-psychologys-most-infamous-experiments/384913/

4 You can read about Robert Rosenthal's work on expectancy effects – which include these studies – as well as many more examples of how both psychologists and participants behave differently when they're involved in psychological studies here: www.psy.gla.ac.uk/~steve/hawth.html

5 Rosenhan, D. L. (1973). On being sane in insane places. *Science*, 179, 250–258. An updated version of this study is reported in Slater, L. (2004). *Opening Skinner's box: Great psychological experiments of the twentieth century*. London: W. W. Norton.

6 Gould, S. J. (1996). *The mismeasure of man*. London: W. W. Norton & Company.

7 Tavris, C. (1991). *The mismeasure of woman: Paradoxes and perspectives in the study of gender*. Washington, DC: American Psychological Association.

8 Sistrunk, F., & McDavid, J. W. (1971). Sex variable in conforming behaviour. *Journal of Personality and Social Psychology*, 2, 200–207.

9 For more on how western psychology has been shaped by history and culture, and how we need to keep attending to these issues, an excellent book is: Jones, D., & Elcock, J. (2001). *History and theories of psychology: A critical perspective*. London: Arnold. A much more recent example demonstrating how psychologists still use their research to endorse problematic practices because of prevailing cultural understandings is the involvement of eminent psychologists in the torture of detainees: www.economist.com/blogs/democracyinamerica/2015/07/terror-torture-and-psychology

10 You might like to compare, for example, the contents pages of Justin Lehmiller's *The psychology of human sexuality* (Oxford: Blackwell, 2014), Chess Denman's *Sexuality: A biopsychosocial approach* (London: Palgrave, 2003), and Christina Richard's and my own *Palgrave handbook of the psychology of sexuality and gender* (Palgrave: London, 2003), all of which are included as further reading in this book. You'd see even more variation if you looked back over the contents pages of psychology of sexuality textbooks over the last century. This is something that Christina and I write more about in this paper: Barker, M., & Richards, C. (2013). What does Bancroft's *Human sexuality and its problems* tell us about current understandings of sexuality? *Feminism & Psychology*, 23(2), 243–251.

11 If you want to you can read more about what these are on my blog at www.rewriting-the-rules.com

12 Spiderman (timeless).

CHAPTER 2

1 Epstein, D., O'Flynn, S., & Telford, D. (2003). *Silenced sexualities in schools and universities*. London: Trentham Books. See www.brainpickings.org/2015/02/16/best-lgbt-childrens-books, corysilverberg.com for some children's books which are trying to be more inclusive.

2 Swearer, S. M., Turner, R. K., Givens, J. E., & Pollack, W. S. (2008). 'You're so gay!': Do different forms of bullying matter for adolescent males? *School Psychology Review*, 37(2), 160.

3 Although we'll come back to some more recent versions of psychoanalysis and what we might usefully learn from them in Chapter 5.

4 Barker, M. (2007). Heteronormativity and the exclusion of bisexuality in psychology. In V. Clarke & E. Peel (Eds.), *Out in psychology: Lesbian, gay, bisexual, trans, and queer perspectives* (pp. 86–118). Chichester, UK: Wiley.

5 Carey, B. (2005). Straight, gay or lying: Bisexuality revisited. *New York Times*, 5.

6 Rieger, G., Chivers, M. L., & Bailey, J. M. (2005). Sexual arousal patterns of bisexual men. *Psychological Science*, 16(8), 579–584.

7 Rosenthal, A. M., Sylva, D., Safron, A., & Bailey, J. M. (2011). Sexual arousal patterns of bisexual men revisited. *Biological Psychology*, 88(1), 112–115.

8 For a review of the research on bisexuality see Barker, M., Richards, C., Jones, R., Bowes-Catton, H., & Plowman, T. (2012). *The bisexuality report: Bisexual inclusion in LGBT equality and diversity*. Milton Keynes: The Open University, Centre for Citizenship, Identity and Governance.

9 Creegan, C. & Keating, M. (2010). *Improving sexual orientation monitoring*. Manchester: Equality and Human Rights Commission. Available from: www.equalityhumanrights.com/sites/default/files/documents/research/improving_sexual_orientation_monitoring_v6_22-12-10.pdf

10 Kinsey, A. C., Pomeroy, W. B., & Martin, C. E. (1948). *Sexual behavior in the human male*. Bloomington: Indiana University Press; Kinsey, A. C., Pomeroy, W. B., & Martin, C. E. (1953). *Sexual behavior in the human female*. Bloomington: Indiana University Press.

11 The film *Kinsey* is a great starting place if you're interested in finding out more about Kinsey's life and work. For details on the research findings see www.kinseyinstitute.org/research/ak-data.html

12 For example, check out the different figures across time and culture on the wikipedia page about sexual orientation: http://en.wikipedia.org/wiki/Demographics_of_sexual_orientation

13 Klein, F., Sepekoff, B., & Wolf, T. J. (1985). Sexual orientation: A multi-variable dynamic process. *Journal of Homosexuality*, 11(1–2), 35–49.

14 Klein, F. (2014). *The bisexual option*. New York: Routledge.

15 Diamond, L. M. (2009). *Sexual fluidity*. Cambridge, MA: Harvard University Press.

16 Chivers, M. L., Seto, M. C., & Blanchard, R. (2007). Gender and sexual orientation differences in sexual response to sexual activities versus gender of actors in sexual films. *Journal of Personality and Social Psychology*, 93(6), 1108.

17 Savin-Williams, R. C., Joyner, K., & Rieger, G. (2012). Prevalence and stability of self-reported sexual orientation identity during young adulthood. *Archives of Sexual Behavior*, 41(1), 103–110.

18 Mock, S. E., & Eibach, R. P. (2012). Stability and change in sexual orientation identity over a 10-year period in adulthood. *Archives of Sexual Behavior*, 41(3), 641–648.

19 Gough, B., & Edwards, G. (1998). The beer talking: Four lads, a carry out and the reproduction of masculinities. *The Sociological Review*, 46(3), 409–455.

20 Pathela, P., Hajat, A., Schillinger, J., Blank, S., Sell, R., & Mostashari, F. (2006). Discordance between sexual behavior and self-reported sexual identity: A population-based survey of New York City men. *Annals of Internal Medicine*, 145(6), 416–425.

21 Haldeman, D. C. (2014). Sexual orientation conversion therapy: Fact, fiction, and fraud. In S. Dworkin & M. Pope (Eds.), *Casebook for counseling: Lesbian, gay, bisexual, and transgender persons and their families*. Hoboken, NJ: Wiley, p. 297.

22 Fausto-Sterling, A. (2000). *Sexing the body: Gender politics and the construction of sexuality*. New York: Basic Books, p. 31. For a simple overview of these ideas see Fausto-Sterling, A. (2012). *Sex/gender: Biology in a social world*. New York: Routledge.

23 Joel, D., Berman, Z., Tavor, I., Wexler, N., Gaber, O., Stein, Y., . . . & Liem, F. (2015). Sex beyond the genitalia: The human brain mosaic. *Proceedings of the National Academy of Sciences*, 112(50), 15468–15473.

24 Fine, C. (2010). *Delusions of gender*. Duxford, UK: Icon Books.

25 Herdt, G. H. (1993). *Third sex, third gender: Beyond sexual dimorphism in culture and history*. New York: Zone Books.

26 Titman, N. (2014). *How many people in the United Kingdom are nonbinary?* www.practicalandrogyny.com

27 Joel, D., Tarrasch, R., Berman, Z., Mukamel, M., & Ziv, E. (2014). Queering gender: Studying gender identity in 'normative' individuals. *Psychology & Sexuality*, 5(4), 291–321.

28 Richards, C., Bouman, W., & Barker, M.-J. (Eds.). (2016). *Genderqueer and non-binary genders*. Basingstoke: Palgrave Macmillan.

29 Bem, S. L. (1981). Gender schema theory: A cognitive account of sex typing. *Psychological Review*, 88(4), 354; Bem, S. L. (1995). Dismantling gender polarization and compulsory heterosexuality: Should we turn the volume down or up? *Journal of Sex Research*, 32(4), 329–334.

30 Barker, M., Richards, C., Jones, R., Bowes-Catton, H., & Plowman, T. (2012). *The bisexuality report: Bisexual inclusion in LGBT equality and diversity*. Milton Keynes: The Open University, Centre for Citizenship, Identity and Governance.

31 METRO Youth Chances. (2014). *Youth Chances summary of first findings: The experiences of LGBTQ young people in England*. London: METRO. There's an overview

of the meaning of different terms here: http://itspronouncedmetrosexual.com/2013/01/a-comprehensive-list-of-lgbtq-term-definitions

32 Bowes-Catton, H., Barker, M., & Richards, C. (2011). 'I didn't know that I could feel this relaxed in my body': Using visual methods to research bisexual people's embodied experiences of identity and space. In P. Reavey (Ed.), *Visual methods in psychology: Using and interpreting images in qualitative research* (pp. 255–270). London: Routledge.

33 Turley, E. L., King, N., & Butt, T. (2011). 'It started when I barked once when I was licking his boots!': A descriptive phenomenological study of the everyday experience of BDSM. *Psychology & Sexuality*, 2(2), 123–136.

34 Sedgwick, E. K. (1990). *Epistemology of the closet*. Upper Saddle River, NJ: Prentice Hall, p. 8.

35 van Anders, S. M. (2015). Beyond sexual orientation: Integrating gender/sex and diverse sexualities via sexual configurations theory. *Archives of Sexual Behavior*, 44(5), 1177–1213.

36 Hegarty, P., & Pratto, F. (2004). The differences that norms make: Empiricism, social constructionism, and the interpretation of group differences. *Sex Roles*, 50(7–8), 445–453.

37 Hegarty, P., & Pratto, F. (2001). Sexual orientation beliefs: Their relationship to anti-gay attitudes and biological determinist arguments. *Journal of Homosexuality*, 41(1), 121–135.

38 Denman, C. (2003). *Sexuality: A biopsychosocial approach*. Basingstoke: Palgrave Macmillan.

39 NATSAL (2013). *Sexual attitudes and lifestyles in Britain: Highlights from Natsal-3*. Available from: www.natsal.ac.uk/media/2102/natsal-infographic.pdf

40 I've written about this in more detail here: http://rewriting-the-rules.com/2014/06/26/will-gay-rights-and-feminist-movements-please-return-to-your-assumptions

CHAPTER 3

1 Barker, M., Gill, R., & Harvey, L. (2018). *Mediated intimacy: Sex advice in media culture*. London: Polity.

2 Masters, W. H., & Johnson, V. E. (1966). *Human sexual response*. Boston: Little, Brown.

3 Kaplan, H. S. (1974). *The new sex therapy*. New York: Brunner/Mazel.

4 American Psychiatric Association. (2013). *DSM-5 – Diagnostic and statistical manual of mental disorders*. Washington, DC: American Psychiatric Association.

5 Kleinplatz, P. J. (2004). Beyond sexual mechanics and hydraulics: Humanising the discourse surrounding erectile dysfunction. *Journal of Humanistic Psychology*, 44(2), 215–242.

6 Hite, S. (1981). *The Hite report: A nationwide study of female sexuality*. New York: Dell.

7 Mintz, L. (2015). The orgasm gap: simple truth & sexual solutions. *Psychology Today*. Available from: www.psychologytoday.com/blog/stress-and-sex/201510/the-orgasm-gap-simple-truth-sexual-solutions

8 Hite, S. (1981). *The Hite report: A nationwide study of female sexuality*. New York: Dell.

9 Potts, A. (2002). *The science/fiction of sex: Feminist deconstruction and the vocabularies of heterosex*. London: Routledge.

10 Potts, A. (2000). 'The essence of the hard on': Hegemonic masculinity and the cultural construction of 'erectile dysfunction'. *Men and Masculinities*, 3(1), 85–103.

11 See Brotto, L. A., Knudson, G., Inskip, J., Rhodes, K., & Erskine, Y. (2010). Asexuality: A mixed-methods approach. *Archives of Sexual Behavior*, 39(3), 599–618.

12 See Carrigan, M. (2015). Asexuality. In C. Richards & M.-J. Barker (Eds.), *Handbook of the psychology of sexuality and gender* (pp. 7–23). Basingstoke: Palgrave Macmillan.

13 NATSAL (2013). *Sexual attitudes and lifestyles in Britain: Highlights from Natsal-3*. Available from: www.natsal.ac.uk/media/2102/natsal-infographic.pdf

14 Barker, M.-J., & Gabb, J. (2016). *The secrets of enduring love: How to make relationships last*. London: Penguin Random House.

15 Tiefer, L. (1995). *Sex is not a natural act*. Boulder, CO: Westview Press.

16 Kleinplatz, P. J. (1998). Sex therapy for vaginismus: A review, critique and humanistic alternative. *Journal of Humanistic Psychology*, 38(2), 51–81.

17 Barker, M. (2011). De Beauvoir, Bridget Jones' pants and vaginismus. *Existential Analysis*, 22(2), 203–216.

18 Kleinplatz, P. J. (2004). Beyond sexual mechanics and hydraulics: Humanising the discourse surrounding erectile dysfunction. *Journal of Humanistic Psychology*, 44(2), 215–242.

19 Yalom, I. D. (2001). *The gift of therapy*. London: Piatkus.

20 Barker, M. (2011). Existential sex therapy. *Sexual and Relationship Therapy*, 26(1), 33–47. p. 40.

21 This was the starting point of the sex advice book which Justin Hancock and I wrote together: Barker, M.-J., & Hancock, J. (2016). *Enjoy sex (How, when and if you want to): A practical and inclusive guide/Sex: A practical guide*. London: Icon Books.

22 Ogden, G. (2001). The taming of the screw: Reflections on 'a new view of women's sexual problems'. In E. Kaschak & L. Tiefer (Eds.), *A new view of women's sexual problems* (pp. 17–22). New York: Haworth. p. 18.

23 Brotto, L., & Barker, M. (Eds.). (2014). *Mindfulness in sexual and relationship therapy.* Abingdon: Taylor & Francis.

24 Mitchell, K. R., Mercer, C. H., Ploubidis, G. B., Jones, K. G., Datta, J., Field, N., . . . & Clifton, S. (2013). Sexual function in Britain: Findings from the third National Survey of Sexual Attitudes and Lifestyles (Natsal-3). *The Lancet*, 382(9907), 1817–1829.

25 Ussher, J. M., & Baker, C. D. (1993). *Psychological perspectives on sexual problems: New directions in theory and practice.* New York: Routledge.

26 Kleinplatz, P. J. (Ed.). (2012). *New directions in sex therapy: Innovations and alternatives.* London: Taylor & Francis.

27 Barker, M.-J., & Gabb, J. (2016). *The secrets of enduring love: How to make relationships last.* London: Penguin Random House.

28 Miller, S. A., & Byers, E. S. (2004). Actual and desired duration of foreplay and intercourse: Discordance and misperceptions within heterosexual couples. *The Journal of Sex Research*, 41, 301–309.

29 Van Hooff, J. (2013). *Modern couples? Continuity and change in heterosexual relationships.* London: Ashgate Publishing, Ltd.

CHAPTER 4

1 You can read more about this – and other – activities in these two essays: Barker, M. (2005). Experience of SM awareness training. *Lesbian & Gay Psychology Review*, 6(3), 268–273; Barker, M. (2007). Turning the world upside down: Developing a tool for training about SM. In D. Langdridge & M. Barker (Eds.), *Safe, sane and consensual: Contemporary perspectives on sadomasochism* (pp. 261–270). Basingstoke: Palgrave Macmillan.

2 There's a longer version of this exercise in the sex chapter of my book: Barker, M. (2013). *Rewriting the rules: An integrative guide to love, sex and relationships.* London: Routledge.

3 American Psychiatric Association. (2013). *DSM-5 – Diagnostic and statistical manual of mental disorders.* Washington, DC: American Psychiatric Association.

4 Barker, M.-J., & Iantaffi, A. (2015). Social models of disability and sex. In H. Spandler, J. Anderson, & B. Sapey (Eds.), *Distress or disability? Madness and the politics of disablement* (pp. 139–152). Bristol: Policy Press.

5 Kutchins, H., & Kirk, S. A. (2003). *Making us crazy.* New York: Simon and Schuster.

6 Moser, C. (2001). Paraphilia: A critique of a confused concept. In P. J. Kleinplatz (Ed.) *New directions in sex therapy: Innovations and alternatives* (pp. 91–108). London: Taylor & Francis.

7 Moser, C., & Kleinplatz, P. J. (2005). Does heterosexuality belong in the DSM. *Lesbian & Gay Psychology Review*, 6(3), 261–267.

8 The journal that Darren Langdridge and I publish, *Psychology & Sexuality*, is one example of this approach and includes many articles taking a non-pathologising and affirmative stance towards the range of sexual identities and practices: www.tandfonline.com/action/journalInformation?show=aimsScope&journalCode=rpse20#.VoPoiMaLTC0

9 Wilson, G. D., & Gosselin, C. (1980). Personality characteristics of fetishists, transvestites and sadomasochists. *Personality and Individual Differences*, 1(3), 289–295; Moser, C., & Levitt, E. E. (1987). An exploratory-descriptive study of a sadomasochistically oriented sample. *Journal of Sex Research*, 23(3), 322–337.

10 Wismeijer, A. A., & Assen, M. A. (2013). Psychological characteristics of BDSM practitioners. *The Journal of Sexual Medicine*, 10(8), 1943–1952.

11 Nordling, N., Sandnabba, N. K., & Santtila, P. (2000). The prevalence and effects of self-reported childhood sexual abuse among sadomasochistically oriented males and females. *Journal of Child Sexual Abuse*, 9(1), 53–63.

12 Renaud, C. A., & Byers, E. S. (1999). Exploring the frequency, diversity, and content of university students' positive and negative sexual cognitions. *The Canadian Journal of Human Sexuality*, 8(1), 17.

13 Durex (2005). *Give and receive: 2005 Global Sex Survey results*. Available from: www.data360.org/pdf/20070416064139.Global%20Sex%20Survey.pdf

14 Barker, M., Iantaffi, A., & Gupta, C. (2007). Kinky clients, kinky counselling? The challenges and potentials of BDSM. In L. Moon (Ed.), *Feeling queer or queer feelings: Counselling and sexual cultures* (pp. 106–124). London: Routledge.

15 Beckmann, A. (2009). *The social construction of sexuality and perversion: Deconstructing sadomasochism*. Basingstoke: Palgrave Macmillan.

16 Kolmes, K., Stock, W., & Moser, C. (2006). Investigating bias in psychotherapy with BDSM clients. *Journal of Homosexuality*, 50(2–3), 301–324.

17 Kleinplatz, P. J., & Moser, C. (Eds.). (2014). *Sadomasochism: Powerful pleasures*. New York: Routledge.

18 Nichols, M. (2006). Psychotherapeutic issues with 'kinky' clients: Clinical problems, yours and theirs. *Journal of Homosexuality*, 50(2–3), 281–300.

19 Barker, M., Gupta, C., & Iantaffi, A. (2007). The power of play: The potentials and pitfalls in healing narratives of BDSM. In D. Langdridge & M. Barker

(Eds.), *Safe, sane and consensual: Contemporary perspectives on sadomasochism* (pp. 197–216). Basingstoke: Palgrave Macmillan.

20 Richards, C., & Barker, M. (2013). *Sexuality and gender for mental health professionals: A practical guide*. London: Sage.

21 Justin Hancock and I talk about how to use theses, and other methods of communicating with yourself and others about sex, in Barker, M.-J., & Hancock, J. (forthcoming, 2016). *Enjoy sex (How, when and if you want to): A practical and inclusive guide*. London: Icon Books. If you're interested in exploring kink specifically then Tristan Taormino's collection is a good starting point: Taormino, T. (Ed.). (2013). *The ultimate guide to kink: BDSM, role play and the erotic edge*. Jersey City, NJ: Cleis Press.

22 Barker, M. (2007). Heteronormativity and the exclusion of bisexuality in psychology. In V. Clarke & E. Peel (Eds.), *Out in psychology: Lesbian, gay, bisexual, trans, and queer perspectives* (pp. 86–118). Chichester, UK: Wiley.

23 Barker, M.-J., Gill, R., & Harvey, L. (forthcoming, 2016). *Mediated intimacy: Sex advice in media culture*. London: Polity.

24 Rubin, R. (2001). Alternative family lifestyles revisited, or whatever happened to swingers, group marriages and communes? *Journal of Family Issues*, 7(6), 711.

25 Vangelisti, A. L., & Gerstenberger, M. (2004). Communication and marital infidelity. In J. Duncombe, K. Harrison, G. Allan, & D. Marsden (Eds.), *The state of affairs: Explorations in infidelity and commitment* (pp. 59–78). Mahwah, NJ: Lawrence Erlbaum Associates.

26 Barker, M., & Langdridge, D. (Eds.). (2010). *Understanding non-monogamies*. New York: Routledge.

27 Conley, T. D., Moors, A. C., Matsick, J. L., & Ziegler, A. (2013). The fewer the merrier?: Assessing stigma surrounding consensually non-monogamous romantic relationships. *Analyses of Social Issues and Public Policy*, 13(1), 1–30.

28 Barker, M., & Langdridge, D. (2010). Whatever happened to non-monogamies? Critical reflections on recent research and theory. *Sexualities*, 13(6), 748–772.

29 Conley, T. D., Ziegler, A., Moors, A. C., Matsick, J. L., & Valentine, B. (2012). A critical examination of popular assumptions about the benefits and outcomes of monogamous relationships. *Personality and Social Psychology Review*, 17(2), 124–141.

30 Sheff, E. (2013). *The polyamorists next door: Inside multiple-partner relationships and families*. London: Rowman & Littlefield.

31 Pallotta-Chiarolli, M. (2010). 'To pass, border or pollute': Polyfamilies go to school. In M. Barker & D. Langdridge (Eds.), *Understanding non-monogamies* (pp. 182–187). London: Routledge.

32 Coontz, S. (2006). *Marriage, a history: How love conquered marriage*. London: Penguin.
33 Holmes, B. M. (2007). In search of my 'one-and-only': Romance-related media and beliefs in romantic relationship destiny. *The Electronic Journal of Communication*, 17(3/4), 1–29.
34 Perel, E. (2007). *Mating in captivity: Unlocking erotic intelligence*. New York: Harper.
35 Sheff, E., & Hammers, C. (2011). The privilege of perversities: Race, class, and education among polyamorists and kinksters. *Psychology & Sexuality*, 2(3), 198–223.
36 Barker, M. (2013). *Rewriting the rules: An integrative guide to love, sex and relationships*. London: Routledge.
37 Heldman, C., & Wade, L. (2010). Hook-up culture: Setting a new research agenda. *Sexuality Research and Social Policy*, 7(4), 323–333.
38 Wosick-Correa, K. (2010). Agreements, rules, and agentic fidelity in polyamorous relationships. *Psychology & Sexuality*, 1(1), 44–61.
39 There's a chapter exploring these continua in depth in Barker, M. (2013). *Rewriting the rules: An integrative guide to love, sex and relationships*. London: Routledge.
40 Ritchie, A., & Barker, M. (2006). 'There aren't words for what we do or how we feel so we have to make them up': Constructing polyamorous languages in a culture of compulsory monogamy. *Sexualities*, 9(5), 584–601.
41 Warren, J.T., Harvey, S. M., & Agnew, C. R. (2011). One love: Explicit monogamy agreements among heterosexual young adult couples at increased risk of sexually transmitted infections. *Journal of Sex Research*, 48(1), 1–8.
42 Barker, M. (2014). Open non-monogamies. In M. Milton (Ed.), *Sexuality: Existential perspectives* (pp. 198–216). London: PCCS Books.
43 Barker, M., Heckert, J., & Wilkinson, E. (2013). Queering polyamory: From one love, to many, and back again. In T. Sanger & Y. Taylor (Eds.), *Mapping intimacies: Relations, exchanges, affects* (pp. 190–208). Basingstoke: Palgrave Macmillan.
44 These were key topics at the non-monogamies conference in 2015. You can view the keynote talks here: http://nmciconference.wordpress.com/keynote-speakers; Nathan Rambukkana also discusses them further in his book: Rambukkana, N. (2015). *Fraught intimacies: Non/monogamy in the public sphere*. Vancouver, BC: UBC Press.
45 If you're interested in finding out more about non-monogamous relationships for your own life then I'd recommend Veaux, F., & Rickert, E. (2014). *More than two: A practical guide to ethical polyamory*. Portland, OR: Thorntree Press, LLC. Some more of my thoughts on where we might take the idea of open relationships are here: http://rewriting-the-rules.com/2014/09/21/open-relationships-revisited

46 Rubin, G. (1984). Thinking sex: Notes for a radical theory of the politics of sexuality. In C. S. Vance (Ed.), *Pleasure and danger: Exploring female sexuality* (pp. 267–319). London: Pandora.

47 Mulholland, M. (2011). When porno meets hetero: SEXPO, heteronormativity and the pornification of the mainstream. *Australian Feminist Studies*, 26(67), 119–135.

48 Mackay, J. (2001). Why have sex? *British Medical Journal*, 322, 623.

49 Hird, M. (2004). *Sex, gender and science*. Basingstoke: Palgrave Press.

50 Roughgarden, J. (2004). *Evolution's rainbow: Diversity, gender, and sexuality in nature and people*. Oakland, CA: University of California Press.

51 Hird, M. (2006). Sex diversity and evolutionary psychology. *The Psychologist*, 19(1), 30–32.

52 Bagemihl, B. (1999). *Biological exuberance: Animal homosexuality and natural diversity*. London: Macmillan.

53 Barash, D. P., & Lipton, J. E. (2001). *The myth of monogamy: Fidelity and infidelity in animals and people*. New York: WH Freeman & Co.

54 Denman, C. (2003). *Sexuality: A biopsychosocial approach*. Basingstoke: Palgrave Macmillan.

55 Jemma Tosh's work is also helpful here as she explores attempts by psychology and psychiatry to include forms of sexual violence as paraphilias over the years: Tosh, J. (2014). *Perverse psychology: The pathologization of sexual violence and transgenderism*. New York: Routledge.

56 The human sexuality map is one example where an author, Franklin Veaux, has tried to imagine what this might look like. It's interesting again to compare this against the DSM delineations of different kinds of sex: www.xeromag.com/sexmap.html

57 Rubin, G. (1984). Thinking sex: Notes for a radical theory of the politics of sexuality. In C. S. Vance (Ed.), *Pleasure and danger: Exploring female sexuality* (pp. 267–319). London: Pandora. p. 283.

58 Barker, M.-J., & Richards, C. (2015). Further genders. In C. Richards & M. Barker (Eds.), *Handbook of the psychology of sexuality and gender* (pp. 166–182). Basingstoke: Palgrave Macmillan.

59 Ministry of Justice, Home Office & the Office for National Statistics (2013). *An overview of sexual offending in England and Wales*. Available from: www.gov.uk/government/uploads/system/uploads/attachment_data/file/214970/sexual-offending-overview-jan-2013.pdf

60 Barker, M.-J., Gill, R., & Harvey, L. (2016). *Mediated intimacy: Sex advice in media culture*. London: Polity.

61 Kitzinger, C., & Frith, H. (1999). Just say no? The use of conversation analysis in developing a feminist perspective on sexual refusal. *Discourse & Society*, 10(3), 293–316; O'Byrne, R., Rapley, M., & Hansen, S. (2006). 'You couldn't say "no", could you?': Young men's understandings of sexual refusal. *Feminism & Psychology*, 16(2), 133–154.

62 Friedman, J., & Valenti, J. (2008). *Yes means yes: Visions of female sexual power and a world without rape*. Berkeley, CA: Seal Press.

63 Beres, M. A. (2007). 'Spontaneous' sexual consent: An analysis of sexual consent literature. *Feminism & Psychology*, 17(1), 93–108.

64 Barker, M. (2013). Consent is a grey area? A comparison of understandings of consent in *50 Shades of Grey* and on the BDSM blogosphere. *Sexualities*, 16(8), 896–914.

65 The Pervocracy (2012). *Consent culture*. Available from: http://pervocracy.blogspot.co.uk/2012/01/consent-culture.html

66 Gavey, N. (2013). *Just sex? The cultural scaffolding of rape*. London: Routledge.

67 Stryker, K. (2017). *Ask: Building consent culture*. Portland, OR: Thorntree Press.

68 Mint, P. (2007). *Towards a general theory of BDSM and power*. Available from: http://freaksexual.wordpress.com/2007/06/11/towards-a-general-theory-of-bdsm-and-power/

69 Weiss, M. (2011). *Techniques of pleasure: BDSM and the circuits of sexuality*. Duke University Press; Bauer, R. (2014). *Queer BDSM intimacies: Critical consent and pushing boundaries*. Basingstoke: Palgrave Macmillan.

70 You can read some more of my thoughts on what broadening out the concept of consent might look like here: http://rewriting-the-rules.com/2014/10/10/consensual-relationships-revisited

CHAPTER 5

1 APA Report. (2007). *American Psychological Association, task force on the sexualization of girls*. Report of the APA task force on the sexualization of girls. www.apa.org/pi/wpo/sexualization.html. Accessed 2 August 2011; Bailey, R. (2011). *Letting children be children*. London: Department for Education. www.education.gov.uk/publications/eOrderingDownload/Bailey%20Review.pdf. Accessed 2 August 2011; Buckingham, D., Willett, R., Bragg, S., & Russell, R. (2010). *External research on sexualised goods aimed at children*. Report to Scottish Parliament Equal Opportunities Committee, SP Paper 374; Byron, T. (2008). *Safer children in a digital world: The report of the Byron Review 2008*. Victoria, BC: DCSF; Papadopoulos, L. (2010). *Sexualisation of young people review*. www.homeoffice.gov.uk/documents/

Sexualisation-young-people. Accessed 2 August 2011; Rush, E., & La Nauze, A. (October 2006). *Corporate paedophilia: Sexualisation of children in Australia*. Canberra: Australia Institute.

2 The 5 *Steps to Tyranny* documentary is a really accessible overview of the psychological research in this area, summarised in this article, and available online: www.theguardian.com/media/2000/dec/19/tvandradio.television1

3 I've written more about the tendency to polarise here: http://rewriting-the-rules.com/2013/06/05/the-tendency-to-polarise/

4 Barker, M.-J. (2012). *50 shades feminist*. Available from: http://rewriting-the-rules.com/2012/07/04/50-shades-feminist/

5 Barker, M.-J. (2014). *The internet and relationships*. Available from: http://rewriting-the-rules.com/2014/11/17/the-internet-and-relationships/

6 Barker, M. (2013). *So monogamy works for some animals. Doesn't mean it's 'natural' for us*. Available from: www.theguardian.com/commentisfree/2013/jul/30/monogamy-animals-evolutionary-research

7 This section is drawn from *The Sexualization Report*: an online resource I was involved with putting together which brings together information and research about sexualization: http://thesexualizationreport.wordpress.com. www.onscenity.org also brings together a number of writers on this topic.

8 e.g. Levin, D., & Kilbourne, J. E. (2008). *So sexy, so soon: The new sexualized childhood and what parents can do to protect their kids*. New York: Ballantine Books; Sarracino, C., & Scott, K. M. (2008). *The porning of America: The rise of porn culture, what it means, and where we go from here*. Boston, MA: Beacon Press.

9 Barker, M., & Duschinsky, R. (2012). Sexualisation's four faces: Sexualisation and gender stereotyping in the Bailey Review. *Gender and Education*, 24(3), 303–310.

10 Hoyle, A. (2012). *Should we panic about pornography?* Available from: www.tes.com/article.aspx?storycode=6287772

11 Bale, C. (2011). Raunch or romance? Framing and interpreting the relationship between sexualized culture and young people's sexual health. *Sex Education*, 11(3), 303–313.

12 His chapter on this in the following book is helpful, and the book as a whole is a good one if you're interested in media impact more broadly. Gauntlett, D. (2008). *Media, gender and identity: An introduction*. London: Routledge.

13 Fine, C. (2010). *Delusions of gender: The real science behind sex differences*. London: Icon Books.

14 Egan, R. D. (2013). *Becoming sexual: A critical appraisal of the sexualization of girls*. London: John Wiley & Sons.

15 Alldred, P., & David, M. E. (2007). *Get real about sex: The politics and practice of sex education*. Maidenhead: Open University Press.
16 Read, J., & Bentall, R. P. (2012). Negative childhood experiences and mental health: Theoretical, clinical and primary prevention implications. *The British Journal of Psychiatry*, 200(2), 89–91.
17 The Sexualization Report can be accessed at: http://thesexualizationreport.wordpress.com
18 Barker, M. (2014). Psychology and pornography: Some reflections. *Porn Studies*, 1(1–2), 120–126.
19 Murnen, S. K. (2015). A social constructivist approach to understanding the relationship between masculinity and sexual aggression. *Psychology of Men & Masculinity*, 16(4), 370–373.
20 Infographic of the day (2014). Hilarious graphs prove that correlation isn't causation. Available from: www.fastcodesign.com/3030529/infographic-of-the-day/hilarious-graphs-prove-that-correlation-isnt-causation
21 Fisher, W. A., & Davis, C. M. (2007). *What sexual scientists know about pornography*. The Society for the Scientific Study of Sexuality. www.sexscience.org/dashboard/articleimages/ssss-pornography.pdf
22 Kutchinsky, B. (1991). Pornography, sex crime and public policy. In S. A. Gerull & B. Halstead (Eds.). *Sex industry and public policy* (pp. 41–54). Canberra: Australian Institute of Criminology.
23 Ferguson, C. J., & Hartley, R. D. (2009). The pleasure is momentary . . . the expense damnable?: The influence of pornography on rape and sexual assault. *Aggression and Violent Behavior*, 14(5), 323–329.
24 Barker, M.-J. (2013). *Studying pornography*. Available from: http://rewriting-the-rules.com/2013/06/01/studying-pornography/
25 Criminal Justice and Immigration Act (2008). Available from: www.legislation.gov.uk/ukpga/2008/4/section/63
26 Ringrose, J., Gill, R., Livingstone, S. & Harvey L. (2012). *A qualitative study of children, young people, and sexting*. London: NSPCC. Available from: www.nspcc.org.uk/globalassets/documents/research-reports/qualitative-study-children-young-people-sexting-report.pdf
27 O'Connor, R. (2013). What does feminist porn look like? *Everyday feminism*. Available from: http://everydayfeminism.com/2013/09/feminist-porn/
28 Fisher, W. A., & Barak, A. (1991). Pornography, erotica, and behavior: More questions than answers. *International Journal of Law and Psychiatry*, 14(1), 65–83.

29 Docz, E. (2015). One lawyer's crusade to defend extreme pornography. *The Guardian*. www.theguardian.com/law/2015/sep/09/one-lawyers-crusade-defend-extreme-pornography

30 Backlash (2015). *Origin story*. Available from: www.backlash-uk.org.uk/origin-story-how-myles-jackman-became-obscenity-lawyer/

31 Bale, C. (2011). Raunch or romance? Framing and interpreting the relationship between sexualized culture and young people's sexual health. *Sex Education*, 11(3), 303–313.

32 Wellcome collection (2015). *Researching pornography*. Available from: http://blog.wellcomecollection.org/2015/06/23/researching-pornography/

33 Short, M. B., Black, L., Smith, A. H., Wetterneck, C. T., & Wells, D. E. (2012). A review of Internet pornography use research: Methodology and content from the past 10 years. *Cyberpsychology, Behavior, and Social Networking*, 15(1), 13–23.

34 Antevska, A., & Gavey, N. (2015). 'Out of sight and out of mind' detachment and men's consumption of male sexual dominance and female submission in pornography. *Men and Masculinities*, 18(5), 605–629.

35 Liberman, R. (2015). 'It's a really great tool': Feminist pornography and the promotion of sexual subjectivity. *Porn Studies*, 2(2–3), 174–191.

36 McKee, A., Albury, K., Dunne, M., Grieshaber, S., Hartley, J., Lumby, C., & Mathews, B. (2010). Healthy sexual development: A multidisciplinary framework for research. *International Journal of Sexual Health*, 22(1), 14–19.

37 McKee, A. (2010). Does pornography harm young people? *Australian Journal of Communication*, 37(1), 17–36.

38 DfEE (2000). *Sex and relationships education (SRE) for the 21st century*. Available from: www.sexeducationforum.org.uk/media/17706/sreadvice.pdf

39 For examples of SRE that does include these things, check out bishtraining.com and www.dosreforschools.com

40 Gauntlett, D. (no date). *Ten things wrong with the media effects model*. Available from: www.theory.org.uk/tenthings.htm

41 Whitworth, A. (2012). Inequality and crime across England: A multilevel modelling approach. *Social Policy and Society*, 11(1), 27–40.

42 Lombard, N. (2013). Violence against women starts with school stereotypes. *The Conversation*. Available from: https://theconversation.com/violence-against-women-starts-with-school-stereotypes-18440

43 See the Everyday Sexism project: www.everydaysexism.com

44 Grabe, S., Ward, L. M., & Hyde, J. S. (2008). The role of the media in body image concerns among women: A meta-analysis of experimental and correlational studies. *Psychological Bulletin*, 134(3), 460; Gill, R. (2009). Mediated

intimacy and postfeminism: A discourse analytic examination of sex and relationships advice in a women's magazine. *Discourse & Communication*, 3(4), 345–369.

45 Horvath, M. A., Hegarty, P., Tyler, S., & Mansfield, S. (2012). 'Lights on at the end of the party': Are lads' mags mainstreaming dangerous sexism? *British Journal of Psychology*, 103(4), 454–471.

46 Burrows, N. (2015). *Responding to the challenge of rape myths in court*. Available from: www.nb-research.com/wp-content/uploads/2015/01/Responding-to-the-challenge-of-rape-myths-in-court_Nina-Burrowes.pdf

47 Simic, Z. (2012). Why 'legitimate' rape and other myths are alive and dangerous. *The Conversation*. Available from: http://theconversation.com/why-legitimate-rape-and-other-myths-are-alive-and-dangerous-8988

48 Reay, B., Attwood, N., & Gooder, C. (2013). Inventing sex: The short history of sex addiction. *Sexuality & Culture*, 17(1), 1–19.

49 Reid, R. C., & Kafka, M. P. (2014). Controversies about hypersexual disorder and the DSM-5. *Current Sexual Health Reports*, 6(4), 259–264.

50 e.g. Carnes, P. (2001). *Out of the shadows: Understanding sexual addiction*. Center City, MN: Hazelden Publishing; Hall, P. (2012). *Understanding and treating sex addiction*. London: Routledge; Maltz, W., & Maltz, L. (2010). *The porn trap: The essential guide to overcoming problems caused by pornography*. New York: William Morrow Paperbacks.

51 Joannides, P. (2012). The challenging landscape of problematic sexual behaviors, including 'sexual addiction' and 'hypersexuality'. In P. Kleinplatz (Ed.), *New directions in sex therapy: Innovations and alternatives* (pp. 69–83). London: Taylor & Francis.

52 COSRT (accessed 2017). *Common sexual problems*. Available from: www.cosrt.org.uk/information-for-members-of-the-public/common-sexual-problems/

53 Tania Glyde usefully unpacks why many of the things often listed as sex addiction are not sex addiction in her blog post here: http://londoncentral-counselling.com/2015/12/02/sex-addiction-what-it-isnt/

54 Davies, D., & Barker, M.-J. (2015). Gender and sexuality diversity (GSD): Respecting difference. *The Psychotherapist*, 60, 16–17.

55 Ley, D. J. (2012). *The myth of sex addiction*. Washington, DC: Rowman & Littlefield Publishers.

56 Irvine, J. M. (2005). *Disorders of desire: Sexuality and gender in modern American sexology*. Philadelphia, PA: Temple University Press.

57 Barker, M. (2013). Reflections: Towards a mindful sexual and relationship therapy. *Sexual Relationship Therapy*, 28(1–2), 148–152.

58 Richards, C., & Barker, M. (Eds.). (2013). *Sexuality and gender for mental health professionals: A practical guide*. London: Sage.

59 Barker, M. (2013). *Mindful counselling & psychotherapy: Practising mindfully across approaches and issues*. London: Sage.

60 Joyal, C. C., Cossette, A., & Lapierre, V. (2015). What exactly is an unusual sexual fantasy? *The journal of sexual medicine*, 12(2), 328–340; Joyal, C. C. (2014). How anomalous are paraphilic interests? *Archives of Sexual Behavior*, 43(7), 1241–1243.

61 A good recent example is Dubberley, E. (2015). *Garden of desires: The evolution of women's sexual fantasies*. London: Virgin Books. The classic Nancy Friday collections are also good, if a little dated now.

62 If you're interested in exploring this out yourself, check out my zine with Justin Hancock: Barker, M.-J., & Hancock, J. (2017). *Understanding ourselves through erotic fantasies*. www.megjohnandjustin.com.

63 Morin, J. (2012). *The erotic mind: Unlocking the inner sources of passion and fulfillment*. London: HarperCollins.

64 Kahr, B. (2006). *Sex and the Psyche: The untold story of our most secret fantasies taken from the largest ever survey of its kind*. London: Allen Lane.

65 Barker, M. (2002). Slashing the slayer: A thematic analysis of homo-erotic Buffy fan fiction. Presentation to the *First Annual Conference on Readings Around Buffy the Vampire Slayer, Blood, Text and Fears*, University of East Anglia, Norwich, 19–20 October 2002. http://oro.open.ac.uk/23340/2/

66 Perel, E. (2007). *Mating in captivity: Unlocking erotic intelligence*. New York: Harper.

67 A helpful book about how people can engage with these kinds of fantasies in their sexual practices is Easton, D., & Hardy, J. W. (2004). *Radical ecstasy: SM journeys to transcendence*. San Francisco, CA: Greenery Press.

68 Chaline, E. (2007). On becoming a gay SMer: A sexual scripting process. In D. Langdridge and M. Barker (Eds.), *Safe, sane and consensual: Contemporary perspectives on sadomasochism* (pp. 155–176). Basingstoke: Palgrave Macmillan.

69 Gagnon, J. H., & Simon, W. (2011). *Sexual conduct: The social sources of human sexuality*. Piscataway, NJ: Transaction Publishers.

70 Cooper, M. (2003). *Existential therapies*. London: Sage.

71 Plummer, K. (1995). *Telling sexual stories: Power, change and social worlds*. London: Routledge.

72 Gill's book is an excellent introduction to the psychology of the media as it relates to gender and sexuality: Gill, R. (2007). *Gender and the media*. Cambridge: Polity.

73 Gill, R. (2003). From sexual objectification to sexual subjectification: The resexualisation of women's bodies in the media. *Feminist Media Studies*, 3(1), 100–106.

74 There's a lot more to these theories of course. If you're interested they're covered in greater depth in: Barker, M.-J., & Scheele, J. (2016). *Queer: A graphic history*. London: Icon Books.

75 Gill, R. (2008). Empowerment/sexism: Figuring female sexual agency in contemporary advertising. *Feminism & Psychology*, 18(1), 35–60.

76 Barker, M., & Gill, R. (2012). Sexual subjectification and Bitchy Jones's diary. *Psychology & Sexuality*, 3(1), 26–40.

77 Barker, M. (2012). *Rewriting the rules: An integrative guide to love, sex and relationships*. London: Routledge.

78 Bad sex media bingo. Available from: http://badsexmediabingo.com